ASTROLOGY OF MONEY

Astrology of Money

Ivarna Kalinkova

Purple Inkwell Publishing

Editor; Edward Henry
email: editor@purple-inkwell.co.uk

isbn: 978-9567454-3-9

To Florence

Always at my side

Contents

IVARNA KALINKOVA 3

INTRODUCTION 10

CHART OF A BILLIONAIRE 1

SELF UNDOING 8

THE ZODIAC SIGNS..12

SUN SIGN ASTROLOGY 30

PLANETS AND SIGNS IN THE 2ND HOUSE. 34

INFLUENCE OF TRANSITS TO SECOND HOUSE..........48

MY FATHERS POCKET 56

THE TRAGEDY OF POVERTY. 62

HEALING AFTER THEFT 64

ASPECTS OF DISHONESTY...78

STOCK MARKET TRADING...82

THE MONEY CHART 94

INTERPRETING THE BUSINESS CHART 96

INCREASE WEALTH WITH MOON CYCLES............102

LUCKY JUPITER 106

PARTNERSHIP OR WORKING FOR YOURSELF 110

THE KARMA OF MONEY..115

KEY TO THE MONEY IN YOUR CHART. 123

MONEY AND INHERITANCE.....................................126

AN INTERESTING CHART 130

HOW TO MAXIMIZE YOUR WEALTH.......................134

TRUTH AND FAILURE 148

LUCK AND ATTRACTING IT. 151

MARS 158

CHART OF A BEGGAR 161

WORK WITH YOUR CHART TO GAIN WEALTH 166

POWER OF PRAYER 172

13 RULES FOR BORROWING MONEY. 188

ASPECTS FROM TRANSITS 196

THE HOUSE NEXT DOOR 202

FAMILY MONEY 203

JUST TELL ME THE WINNING NUMBERS 205

AVOID LIVING OTHER PEOPLES DREAMS.................218

RULES OF ANALYSIS 223

SUMMARY 229

Introduction

Astrology of Money, how to attract wealth, using both simple and complex astrology and spiritual techniques. Exploring wealth and poverty astrologically. To recognize false and dangerous mythologies that will make you poorer. To increase your wealth. The Karma of money, the loss and the gains.

We are not all born wealthy but we are all born with the ability to be richer than we are. The book is about financial astrology, it is interlaced with a series of esoteric and spiritual steps to increase your wealth. The two things work together for best results, but both can be used separately. The book also contains a few interesting astrological charts and examples. How wealth, poverty, debts, losses and gains show in the chart. How to predict your own financial fortunes. This book is suitable both for beginners, and those with a much more complex knowledge of astrology.

How do you know if Jupiter, the giver of money, will bring good or bad luck? How do you know if your Moon in the second house will work positively like Richard Branson's Moon, or negatively and cause debts and downfall?

The book also assumes that you can "Chart read". That is to say look at your own chart or another person, and recognize the symbols for the planets, and which planet is in which house and sign. This is all you need to know. You can obtain your own Natal chart free from many websites.

I am not trying teach you all about astrology here, but to make you think for yourself, it is not meant to detail every sign, planet, every configuration of stars. I aim to reveal some things, provide you with the tools of knowledge and leave you to work out the rest for yourself. What you learn will be unique because of part of it comes from within you.

It is also a book intended to make you think about money and to help you get richer. The wealth that I wish for you is good financial wealth but also spiritual wealth and worldly security and happiness to go with it. To have the freedom money can give without the shackles and yokes and unhappiness it sometimes brings. To have wealth, wisdom, freedom and strength. You can have each one without the other, but when you have all four, you are truly enriched. It can take as much inner strength to survive being rich without losing your essential self, or direction, as it can to survive being poor, remember that, it is an essential truth.

Chart of a Billionaire

If there is a fate to be poor, then there is also fate to be rich. These are two unmarked and interchangeable doors of possibility Both lead into the future, they stand side by side in the same vestibule in the house of your life. By one or more steps you will stumble blindly forward in time to the rich room or the poor room, never knowing quite how you got there except it was somehow ordained by fate. But what if you could *choose* the door? What if you could walk the path to wealth, step by step? once you know the way you can turn from one door to the other at any time in your life. It is often assumed that there is an incalculable difference between the chart of a wealthy man and that of a poor man. But this is not so the difference is infinitesimally small. I have worked in astrology many years. I have scrutinized the charts of people who have made more wealth in their life time than there is sand on a beach, and looked with equal interest at the charts of those whose food and shelter are scavenged from the milk of human kindness and the crumbs of necessity. The rich man's chart and the beggars chart, are not identical, but they are as inseparable as any one chart is from another. It is within the power of any one of us to rise to become rich, It is within the power of any one of us to sink into poverty.

When I look at an astrological chart I can often see how fate like a restless wind has tried to enhance the persons life both with good fortune happiness and money, and how it has all blown away, swept aside like autumn leaves on a tiled path, never to materialize. That they should have been rich a long time ago. But something has blocked it, or decreased the power of the aspects in the past, or money has slipped through their hands like a ghost. I see charts of people who have been cheated. Of wasted wealth, lost fortunes, missed opportunities, and the latter is the one that makes me grieve most, how through the years the diminishing power of wealth withers like a frosted plant, when it could be so fine and abundant, with just a little more attention to the stars. It is as though there is a rich road for all of us, but we miss the turning, or are misled down Losers Alley, and are robbed of our chances, our potential along with our money. I see talent go un-rewarded, when fame and fortune goes to someone else of lesser ability. I see it all. But what I also notice is that wealth, when it comes, is a road we only stagger along, on into the dark, not quite knowing how we got there, the door that opens, then closes, and is otherwise invisible to us. Yet it need not be. We can all, with the help of astrology, find the way there, and find the way back again, we can all fill our pockets to overflowing with the gold that is rightfully ours, and with that wealth we can do infinite good in the world. Your chart is your advisor and your sign post.

The first chart I present in this book is of a popular billionaire and philanthropist. This mans chart is not so very different from your own or that of your closest friends, but he is mega millionaire and you are not, So why hasn't this happened to you? More importantly how can we make it happen?

We are not all born rich but we are born with the ability to be richer than we are.

Richard Branson's choice of business name seems curious and inspired, and fated. The sign of Virgo the Virgin was on Mr. Branson's house of money at birth, His own ruling planet the Moon was on the cusp of that house. The Moon has to do with fame, recognition, and his brand name Virgin is world famous. But what makes his chart different to any one of us? The answer is, it isn't. Traditionally the Moon is often considered to be a weak and negative potential in the house of money, it's the sign of the wanderer and the wastrel, but the charismatic Mr Branson has drawn on it's strength not on it's weakness. He has used his charts potential correctly. Any one of us can use our charts hidden potential correctly and become a multi millionaire, or at least improve our finances so we can use the gifts written in our fate (our chart) wisely.

Richard was born under the zodiac sign of Cancer, his Sun is in the twelfth house, the house of hidden potential. and in true twelfth house fashion he began life unknown and in obscurity. His power in business was for a long time faceless, anonymous, a man behind the scenes. His twelfth house cancer Sun is a shy, vague, and hidden Sun,. My reason for choosing this chart, is at fist glance it is not a very auspicious one.

The Sun influences the physical appearance, it gives a boyish or eternal student type shadow and a vibrancy hidden behind his looks, and Cancer in youth has something of the "Boy next door" appeal. while his Pluto ascendant in Leo, gives the leonine like charisma, Leo his sandy mane and beard. In advanced old age this same aspect will also give

3

him spinal trouble and a stoop. He has Pluto just below his ascendant. The ascendant is one's birth. Pluto can be sudden destructive and deadly or it can be a wonderful planet, again the two sides of the same door. On the ascendant it gives the ability to transform ones life from what it was at birth into something more extreme.

Pluto can drop you to the depth or raise you to the heights and it will seem like destiny but it's really the path you have chosen. Richard chose the right door. Pluto is the phoenix planet, it gives the innate ability to rise from the dregs and ashes if you crash. Should Richard have gone bankrupt, he'd have had the potential to start again from nothing, rising like a rocket.

Like many rich famous people Richard is portrayed as beginning with nothing. This is actually not true, he came from a middle class background and had a university education., with all the usual privileges that middle class parenting and education bring.

It's hardly "nothing". Those who regard it as such don't know what coming from nothing really means. So he was dealt a better hand than many at birth. We don't begin life on an even playing field, yet he has risen far higher than others with a similar comfortable background. More importantly for our illustration he has been able to turn his chart over to it's utmost advantage.

Richard's Career began in college. His Mars, ruler of his house of Career sits in the house of education. This is appropriate since one of his early entrepreneurial ventures was a student magazine. Aries is the first sign of Spring, it tends to make things happen in youth and the Spring-time of life.

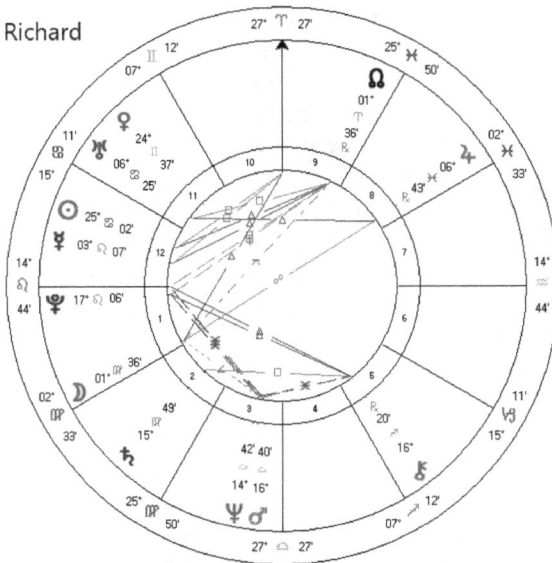

Richard

Here is a picture of someone young enthusiastic. Not all that studious, academic or scholarly, but ambitious. This is sign that could so easily have applied not to Richard but to someone who evades responsibility, drops out of college, who wants to work, or rather play at work, hangs around and has fun at college, not dedicating himself to the serious study of anything, since escapist Neptune sits in the house of education. So it is not special aspect, not a rich mans aspect. He could have taken the alternative door, turned into a middle class drop out, used all the chart energy's negatively and been a wastrel, who only played at life. But it's a youthful aspect. It is given strength by Mars Sextile to Pluto rising (the ability to transform ones life) and by Neptune conjunct Mars. Neptune is a dream. Mars is the energy and strength to fight to make that elusive dream into reality. So what Richard's chart shows then, when read positively instead of negatively, is a youthful dream, a visionary that had the ability to take off and transform his life.

The planets mean different things at different times in life. If we come back to his third house, Neptune, this student dream, we see the other third house meanings of the stars. The third house is journeys and transport, the goings back and forth in life,. Neptune's is long distances, Virgin airways and trains, another image another time, reflected in the same aspect.,.

The dream began with a telephone box, a student magazine and with music; Virgin records. Neptune can be music. But what connects the escapist planet with Virgo on the house of money? The answer is Saturn, at the midpoint between Pluto and Mars. Hard work attention to detail, necessity and endurance, fear of financial loss though Jupiter in his eighth house shows favourable financial trends that would always rescue him from hardship. Richard's Saturn means he worked hard at his dream, there was an element of luck, Jupiter, but this chart is still ordinary. It is not an unusual chart. In medicine the same substances can kill or cure, only the way they are used is different. It is the same in astrology. Some people gain their fortune through pure luck. Some by winning the lottery. Or by an un-hoped for inheritance, a kind benefactor. Some have a good idea or an opportunity that changes everything. But what Richard did and what those who succeed in a spectacular way do that many of us don't ever manage to do, is instinctively or unknowingly use all the potential in the chart, all the positive aspects and tides of life in his chart to advantage and he avoided the dark door, the negative side of the chart.

The negative side would be having been this; Moon in second house indicates debts, fluctuations, uncertainty. Saturn in the Second house which can mean poverty, destitution, or fear of change. Pluto close to the ascendant, the possibility of bad extremes, bankruptcy. Sun in twelfth, inability to rise through life's difficulties. No planets in tenth, no direction in career. But he utilized, perhaps from instinct, perhaps from some inner fate. the positive side of all the planets, never the negative. So his success was as spectacular as his failure might have been. He became mega rich.

This book aims to help you do the same. To know what is in your chart, to use it positively, and to bring out your own great and hidden potential for wealth. It will answer the question why when your chart has a much potential as this man, aren't you wealthy, it may even make you just as wealthy!

Self Undoing

A first step in overcoming the psychology and karma that binds people to poverty; Working too hard for money, Poverty consciousness. Saturn in the chart.

Mental traps of attitude undermine your success. A tangle of false beliefs and subconscious notions that drag you down beneath the waters of poverty and stop you rising and gaining wealth, an example is when we subconsciously equate wealth with reward for good behavior, and poverty as a punishment. When you feel deep down that you haven't gained the thing you desire because you have not yet earned that thing, or have not worked hard enough. This can be Negative Saturn influences, Saturn aspecting the midheaven, Saturn or Capricorn rising. The subconscious notion that everything must be hard earned. This acts as a block to wealth. In the chart of self made people, these aspects are also often prominent but they work in positive way, instead of acting as a block they spur the person on to succeed and rise from nothing.

Never underestimate the strength of the subconscious mind, it can steer you towards a wealthy path or a bare one. Only when you are free of such notions is soul free to guide you to wealth.

Perhaps you think you work hard enough but your not a good enough person to be blessed or rewarded by fate with money, or you think your talent and skill are worthless, and you feel that this is why God made you too poor to prosper. If so then look for afflictions to the ascendant and Sun, when this personal mentality of feeling inferior can be overcome then wealth will eventualy follow. When we change or mend the inner self, we attract a different better fate, we heal the source of the poverty in our life. A man once said to me, there are many fates but only one destiny. He was right.

There can be many roads to the same city, we can choose a poor one, and a cart track made of dust and cobbles, or one paved with coins and gold. Saturn affliction may be hardest to change, but they can be wrestled into wealth, once you stop believing all the lies that people told you about yourself when you were young; Saturn in the past, a history of being made to feel worthless, that you were unimportant, that your thoughts and feeling didn't mater. That you had no value and deserve nothing better than you have. That you deserve to be treated this way. The outer world reflects the inner. Once you stop believing that you are worthless, you are a step towards self healing and a step towards money. Negative influences from Neptune are operating when you think you have given nothing up, to gain wealth. That you haven't sacrificed enough, when your soul has' martyred itself or bled enough on the hard stones of life. That you haven't suffered enough for the reward to come. These are lies. Or alternatively if you think that money is wrong, bad, or unspiritual, that self denial is good for the soul. That the saint and the prophet and the good person are always poor. These are foolish philosophy's and if your subconscious believes in them it will hold you back. A way to overcome the Neptune mentality within you, is to think that with money you can do good for others or the world without denying yourself luxury in the process. But without money you can do nothing Think of good people who are wealthy, and wealthy people who have done good (once again Mr Branson is a great example). This will re-train your subconscious thoughts, so that they don't precede actions that steer you down the "Losers" path. Fix that in your mind like a motto. The more you have, the more to give and make things good. Once the subconscious gets this message it will steer your path towards a more monied one.

Jupiter is supposed to be a good planet who gives abundance, but if you think you are unlucky, or other people have all the luck (negative Jupiter), that other people gain too easily, or make no effort but come off better than you. If you think misfortune is to blame, then it is not those people that matter, what you think is what counts. To help overcome the negative Jupiter you have to revise your attitude that success and wealth are down to pure chance, Wealth is always in part down to yourself. Luck is the icing on the cake, the random sweetness. But a person can always make himself richer and in the process attract or increase his own luck too.

Astrologically afflictions to Jupiter, may manifest in "bad luck", because the spirit. unconsciously does things at the wrong time, or misses good opportunities.

Uranus in negative aspects feels circumstance is against him. The recession ruins the business, the times were not right, he has had a bad start. He is born disadvantaged. It is not in his fate to have money. The shadow side of Uranus is about believing the misguided dangerous philosophy's of shifting the blame, onto fate, or other people, or the terms we live if. If you don't find where you went wrong or own your own part in going wrong, then, how can you find where to go right? The affirmation that counters this lie, is I am stronger than fate. I am master of my own destiny. I will rise.

There are traps and other lies we tell ourselves, they are all a false philosophy, look around you, there are many people so good in heart that they should never suffer the degradation of poverty at all, people such with such vision that they should have the money to make the dream reality and make the world a better place for us all;. And there are also people who are nasty mean, spiteful and hurtful and evil beyond measure, and have more money that anyone could use squander in a hundred life times. People who have wealth but use it only to perpetuate harm and evil and gain more, and people whose money is bad, rotten from the roots, who don't mind how it is obtained, or what has suffered or been destroyed in the process. Carrion crows and Vultures profit. Rats win the rat race. Money has no judgement of it's own and it has nothing to do with justice or goodness, and it has only a modicum to do with luck, or chance. Do not allow false morals and wrong judgments to blind you and to cloud your senses. Every false belief like this is a chain that limits your outlook, and pins you more heavily into poverty. Aim to make a better reality by all means, but at least see reality first, because if you don't you're a rabbit on the railway line, and as soon as you begin to make money, first one vulture, then another will appear.

Morals and money are not connected untill we connect them. It is better for your spirit and the world around you and your karma for you to get rich and thrive in a good way. A way that doesn't involve the suffering of others, or cause other peoples hardship, loss and exploitation, or cause the depletion of the planet., it's plants and it's animals. If you have no scruples, and make the gain of money the totality of life, you will miss much of life's texture, or will fall by the wayside into the evil paths of greed and destructive desire and the price you'll pay for money will be too high for what you get back. The real treasure will be lost, and you will be lost to yourself. But don't be fooled into thinking that reward and punishment, good and evil are connected to money. They are not. Whether you like that truth or not, it is a good place to begin, The truth let's illusion fall away like a garment from your shoulders, so it no longer burdens you, no longer snags on things as you walk freely forward. The rich are no better than the poor, in this life or any other, if it worry's you, make yourself a promise that when your wealthy you will be better than them. keep that promise, because it's a promise to your soul, your deeper self.

Later in the book we will be looking at some more of these mental traps, and the astrology and psychology of it in your chart, with the aim of setting you free of them. The natal chart is like a door, it has two sides. We can live life through the negative side of the chart or the positive side, the worst side or the best. The evil within us, or the good within us. This book will not only help you become richer but it will enable you to acquire wealth in a spiritually acceptable and good way.

The Zodiac Signs

The zodiac sign is the constellation that the Sun is transiting through at the time of your birth. The word "zodiac " means circle of animals, the word zoo derives from the same root. Some of the zodiac signs are creatures, like the goat, or half creatures like the Sagittarius, some are ancient goddesses, like the Virgin, each symbol has different story, but they all symbolise a sacred circle of life. The transiting Sun is the symbol of life awakening, the season and times changing on earth and a symbol of birth, or creation, therefore it's a symbol of the self. The zodiac signs are the most basic level of astrology, if you know nothing else you already know your zodiac sign and it's attributes. In financial astrology the zodiac sign has only a limited influence., It shows how your character and circumstance of your birth have shaped your attitude to wealth and the gaining of money.

ARIES

If you have Aries as your zodiac sign, you have good earning powers combined with tremendous need for money, influence and popularity, but difficulty obtaining it. You look up to wealth and admire the rich. Money for you is a means of popularity, independence, show and security. To buy what you want in life. You like possessions that you can flaunt, the trappings of wealth and luxury. You like to win, to have more than others in your circle. But you are not too good at handling your money, you can have it spent before you've got it. You are direct and honest in your dealings, but money goes out too rapidly. Comes in too slow. You often have a " cash flow" problem. You have an enterprising spirit. Attracted to get rich quick ideas, and risk taking with what you have, you are gullible you find it hard to save and tend to dip into the savings. Long term investments with slow returns don't hold much appeal. You seem to need quick results. You can save up quickly if you see something you want to buy. But find it harder just to set money away for savings, if there is no particular aim for the savings.

You are extravagant, generous, and careless. You like to spend money on modern possessions, state of the art things, and up to the minute devices. You like to show that you have more than others.

You are usually lucky in money making and can rake in a fast return on what you put out. You are good at business, and at inventing money making schemes and putting them into action. You have a strong sense of direction and good ideas, much ambition, and the confidence to push ahead against obstacles in your path and against other people negativity, even if you have to start at the bottom, you will persevere and struggle to proudly obtain the worldly things you want. You can make your money grow, but you usually find some new thing to spend it on, or some new expense, so as the years go on, it doesn't pile up a great deal. You just cannot stop working, and spending. You have the energy required to become rich, and the luck, but you also need to develop far sightedness, in providing for the future, you live too much for the moment. Buy now, pay later appeals. The eternal optimism of what good luck or rescue might befall you in years to come.

TAURUS

Born under Taurus the starry Bull, you are motivated by a physical need for material and financial comfort, ease and well being in your life. You like money, you like to savour what feeling rich is like. Money can heal your wounds from life. You buy expensive possessions that give you pleasure because of their beauty as well as for their material worth. You like owning things. You have beautifull clothes and expensive Jewelry. Objects of beauty in your home. You spend money on music, fine art or craftwork. Also food luxuries. These things give you pleasure. You have a desire more for the wealthy lifestyle and possessions to enjoy owning more than for money itself. You can be self indulgent and a spendthrift, but you are shrewd and wise and not wasteful with money all the same.

You hang on to property and goods once you obtain them, and you have a strong need to have a nice solid home in it's own ground or garden. Possessive about material passions and down to earth. You make money slowly and surely, you have stamina and can work hard and endure hardship. Your ideas that make you money are not always total originally or inovative, you often improve on existing things, rather than invent or create, but the way you can make something better, or more profitable is good. You don't make rash or unwise decision about money, but you can be stubborn, staid and inflexible, immovable when people push you. You are patient, and can wait for returns and profits on investments. You are generous and spend, but you also set something aside for harder times too. You are the most sensible of signs. Money can come to you from favours from others, from being liked. And money is spent on friends and social life, it comes it goes but never completely. At the very worst you have enough, at the very best your cups or coffers brim over. This is a materialistic practical sign, and earth sign with a down to earth attitude and winning ways.

GEMINI

Money will occupy much of your thoughts and your interests. Gemini means you are clever or crafty when it comes to money. You must seek to improve your earnings by use of your shrewd sharp wits. You have a mind, this is quick to make connections between things, quick to see where there might be a gain for you. The gain in your life may be connected with learning and books and education. Or adversely with a different kind of intelligence, being cunning, sneaky, sly inventive and conniving. But either way you will gain your wealth by your own ingenuity. Some people born under Gemini have finances and income that is bound up with relatives, or friends. You are involved in many different schemes and interests, and financial activities. You are likely to have more than one bank account or credit card. You have financial acumen but a tendency to hesitate or delay or to be afraid of taking on heavy financial commitments, though you live for the day with little thought of debts piling up tomorrow. You take action when you have to. This can cause set backs, or to miss the opportunity for financial success. You want money but are equally afraid of responsibilities that sometimes go with it.

You are adaptable to wealth and poverty. You can be inventive and can turn you hand to anything, regardless of weather you have had any training or experience, you can do all things, or you think you can, but are an expert in none. When it comes to making money, you are flexible, you adjust and adapt to what is required of you, You assert yourself well in discussion and have good business sense, some would say you're a natural salesperson, persuasive and able to enlist the cooperation of others. You would like money without effort, so it's the mind you mostly apply to increasing your money. You are interested din other peoples money, and observant, how much they earn, what they do, how they spend, what way if gaining money has worked for them, that might work for you. You collect ideas and information that are useful to your money making skills. You don't put all your financial eggs in one basket. You spread your savings and investments in various ways so that one disaster cannot wipe the lot out. You take risks, you set traps, you are not scrupulous, not totally honest and your risks are usually calculated ones. You are flexible and ever ready for change in your life.

CANCER

Being born under the zodiac sign of Cancer, security is a deep emotional need and your attitude to money will be serious, because money means security to you, without it you are anxious and sad. You always show great maturity in handling your money and can be much wiser than others in your family and home in financial affairs. This is not a sign that attracts wealth though, but you have a knack of hanging on to what money you have, without being mean or miserly in the process of keeping it safe..

You take an interest in others, in how the rich and famous manage their financial affairs. Or in how national changes and government policy's affect your own income and money. You do not like to run short of money and the effect on your emotional well being when you do is a dramatic and deep misery. Once you are aware of this money-mood link, you will take a greater interest in your financial affairs. You are reluctant to part with savings or money you have set aside, once sunk into the bank vault or your hidey hole it doesn't easily come out to se the light of day again, you are not mean, just carefull. If you do part with money it is always for a very good cause or need. You tend to hoard things, including money, possessions and are reluctant to throw anything away, because it all have a value, or use. You have a talent for reusing things and getting the most wear out of a thing, You store things up for another occasion

You like value for money, quality and endurance. You like to keep money safe, so you may not carry much cash. But you find learning to deal with banks and other investment houses is a difficult concept, and the complexities of financial matters, mortgages, loans, interests insurances, savings plans will at times perplex you. You like things simple and straight forwards. and secure. You are not a risk taker. You may have more than one bank account as you like to keep your money in different compartments, some Cancerains have one bank account for savings, one for regular spending money, and another for a special purpose. When you give, you do so generously, without strings or conditions, and without expecting anything in return. You pay your debts and keep your promises to others financially. You build up a supportive family, strong friends or a good emotional background pleasant relationship with the professional people you have to deal with financially and contacts, bank managers and so on, from which you can draw support, money and help in times of difficulty.

LEO

You like to make a show of having a fancy or extravagant lifestyle. Of being good hearted and immensely free and generous,, but underneath you know where and how every penny is spent and how liberal you can afford to be. Money and possession are something like to keep carefull watch on. Sauce for the goose isn't sauce for the gander. You will argue in a fiercely penny pinching way, with your dependents and partners over their unnecessary expenditures and then go out and buy something lavish yourself. You are inconsistent financially. You are generous with others when they have earned your respect or when you want to be appreciated by them,. You expect gratitude, or admiration and become mean and critical or hurt when it's not given. However you are susceptible to flattery and much money can be wasted on hangers on who have paid you compliments.

You are shrewd and discerning when it come to property and large financial resources. You take good care if your investments, to se they don't depreciate in value. You make sure that insurance premiums are paid up and bills settled and that property and vehicles are kept in good repair. You worry about money more than admit, and your anxieties can make you ill, you will fight to the last to hang onto what you have and own. You are not so good at accepting financial help from others, you'd rather have advice, so you can put it to good use to help yourself win through. Winning, being solvent, having a wealthy image are almost more important to you than wealth itself. You appear carelessly extravagant, but are shrewder than you seem. When you have nothing to tend to hide your poverty as if it was a shameful habit, making excuses for yourself, or ducking out of social commitments where you may have to spend more than you can afford, rather than letting others carry the bill for once. You have vision of wealth and what you would do with it, but cannot always plan how to get to that stage.

VIRGO

You are realistic and cautious when it comes to financial affairs. Many Virgos are methodical in their accounting and run their personal budgets and finances with punctuality and precision, You are fault finding and thrifty. During your life time, hard responsible word will pay off for you. Highly organised. Anxious about being ill, or incapable, about having to take time away form work, or about financially affairs going wrong. You worry more than most about eventuality's and the pressures of obligation and responsibilities. You often have debts but rarely are they beyond your control. You balance the books well and are carefull but not miserly. You like to take care of others and to have the money to do that. You are conscientious about paying your share of things, or giving, and you notice when others don't., even if you don't protest out loud, it is all noted down

You are clever and quick at making money and can analyze what went wrong when you failed to make it and usually put it right This sign is good at making money from things dear to your heart, labors of love, if you love a thing enough you can make it work. Virgo is also associated with hard work in subordinate positions and service positions. You are mostly solvent and able to manage your own money well. But you would like to be better off. Conscientious with other people's money, you are able to get them the best deals and help them when they place their financial trust in you. You give good impartial financial advice and research the details, the small print. You are able to help people correct their mistakes and muddles. You are equally good at cooking the books, and covering up and hiding your own financial mistakes and indiscretions. Everyone thinks you don't make mistakes, that you're wiser or better, more upright than you are in handling your finances.

Self denial when it's necessary is not too difficult for you. You face hardships with fortitude. Neither is it hard for you to making financial commitments. You are sensible with your generosity, not extravagant. You help the needy but prefer to help them towards their own financial independence, rather than just giving. You have long term goals and you can stick to them, saving and investing carefully, well informed, you get the deals. You are not extravagant and you don't get pleasure from taking risks.

LIBRA

This sign attracts security and comfort rather than wealth. However it favours others as a source of finance, or a means to supplement ones own money rather than ones own earnings. Libra usually makes a comfortable income through long hours of industrious labour, but some Libras end up being kept and not having to work. The income is usualy supplemented by parents, a partner, a help mate or other sources of income that you come to depend on. You don't do so well on your own, though you'd like to think you do. You feel yourself to be independent but you aren't. You live humbly but not frugally, you are sensible and saving and you don't waste things. You worry about financial security, and are suspicious or fearfull about loss and deceit. Your not trusting, you don't trust even when you should, but you are still not able to avoid money and shortages problems for long.

You are more generous to those you love than to yourself, you spend more on presents for others, than you'd spend on yourself. You have a sacrificial side, a self denying side and will go without or endure hardship to give to others who are close to you more. You are fair, generous, honest, you pay what you owe, and are willing to compromise in money matters. You don't like disputes or having to ask for money or assert yourself about money. For this reason you sometimes just let things go. You don't always correct mistakes or collect money owed to you when there is going to be trouble about it. But you don't forget it either. Once you feel you have been wronged financially, you don't deal with that person or company ever again.

Your strong impulse is to spend money on beautifull things. You buy things that last, furniture property good clothes, and they have to last a long time, if you have spent money on a thing you will get your value or wear out of it. You will have it for years. But often you cannot earn enough for the things you would like to have, and may depend on others. You are routinely giving or generous, you give when it's expected, a birthday gift and so on.

But you never give on impulse or for no reason. You save by cutting down on things, and by lack of extravagance but there are many contradictions. You are a person who would be unhappy living a hard life, or unhappy in poor surroundings, but may find yourself there, even when you could be wealthier, because you are not adaptable, you don't change things radically. You sent move on. The coat is warm when it's new, but you still cleave to it when it's threadbare and cold. Your stubborn inability to change holds you back from affluence, which is like a tide you have to move with it, or float on it. You cannot stand still and retain what you had, it doesn't work. Time moves on without you. You have average luck in gambling and speculation but not abundant luck. You life is like a slow wheel of fortune. You go up, you reach the peak, and then you go gradually down.

SCORPIO

Born under the constellations of Scorpio. People wonder where your money comes from. Your sources of income are not always known to others. Money is important to you, because subconsciously you see money as a form of power, and a form of control. Some Scorpios work and amass money because money gives them control over their lives, or independence. This may be what you want. The desire to work for yourself and which you would be good at. Some Scorpios amass money because it gives them control over other people, even if it is only being the one to hold the purse strings in a relationship. It is not greed that motivates a Scorpio to want wealth. It is to do with power and control. Most Scorpios are successful at making money, but, once they have found their right karmic vocation.

The thing they were born to do. Not always before that.

Where money is concerned you are astute and intelligent. You hide your interest and desire for money, under a façade of seeming to consider other more spiritual or unworldly things more important than money. You rise to the top of your chosen field, though you prefer to rule from behind the scenes. Scorpio's tend to come into money from inheritance, this can happen early in life, so long as no malefic planets are in your sign to delay prevent it., Your money is greatly influenced by the money or lack of money of a partner those close to you.

There is a mean and penny pinching streak in you. You are only generous to those you love a great deal. People with this sign often end up as work horses, which carry their partners and family financially. Keeping the money is keeping the power. Giving it, is giving away power, so you may also find that you are not a generous person. I have actually only known one generous Scorpio, a female, but she used sex as power and as a sort of currency instead. You can be ambitious and singled minded, you never give up on your original vision, and when you earn success or wealth by it, the wealth and success endures. You keep secrets, including financial ones, and secrets that give you power over others. You are not afraid to take big risks for big gains.

Few people will know how much you are worth, or how much you have salted away in savings and investments. You prefer it that way, not because you're dishonest, but because you are mistrustful of others and of how they may use what they know about you. There is a ruthless streak with money and business. You fear people will beg, or borrow or thieve from you. You are not a starship who likes to carry passengers. Without money you fear you have no power, no adequacy, or independence.

You pay your debts, and are mostly honest, but survival and self preservation comes first financially.

SAGITTARIUS

Your financial outlook is colored by optimism and faith in the future to bring you the wealth you deserve. You are one of the zodiac signs that has a degree of luck. You make the right decisions, take the right risks, because you are intuitive where money or making it, or winning it is concerned. You also have good economic understanding and vision for the future. You are wise and understand the trends, you se the big picture in finances, as well as the small individual one and you know the way things are going. You also have a deep faith in providence, that when you need it something will come along, some lucky turn of events to see you round the difficult corner, and usually it does. You think of it as good fortune but it's partly your own skills.

Most of the time you will have an above average income, or will be able to live as though you have.

You are generous to other people and magnanimous in money matters. Even if you are not wealthy you have a way of behaving and living that makes other people think you are wealthier. Wealth sometimes attracts wealth, so you grow in prosperity. It is as though riches or a better life would come easily to you, as though you were born to have a greater wealth than you actually have. The older you get the more you will have.

Easy come, easy go is a feature of your financial life, your money flows, but the tides that wax can also wane., there will spells of hardship. You don't think in trifling sums, or small change, your sights are set on the main picture. You have confidence in your decision and in your inner resourcefulness to pull through when they go wrong. Legal matters, travel, education religion and charity's, speculation and gambling all have an influence on your financial life. You may earn your living from a wide variety of occupations and you can be lucky Chances will pay off for you, you know when to risk things, when not. You will also have lucky windfalls from time to time. Money helps your Moon, you feel despondent when going through a poor patch, and your main aim in having money is to feel good, and live better, to enjoy your wealth and the good life and colourfull wide experiences that money can bring.

CAPRICORN

You are frugal, ambitious, responsible and practical with money. You take things slowly and steadily and generally speaking you will rise gradually throughout your life to a better wealthier position. You will acquire things that have lasting value. You can be economic, miserly, money grabbing and detached. When you spend money you like value for it, or to the most out of a situation for your investment. If you take a fancy iced cake to a friend's house for tea, you'll claw back the price of it, when you talk her into being a free baby minder, taxi, or hotel for your weekend. This form of economy comes natural to you. You can be, stingy and frugal, you give the minimum and extract the maximum. you make sure you get a return on all your investments. You tend to be economic and saving in some things in order to amass money to spend on others,. You skimp on necessities, to buy luxuries.

You have endurance and can patiently work away and wait for wealth to materialize. You have steady earnings which can be slow and limited, but will increase with time. You know how to extract something from nothing, something for free. You make money go a long way and you dislike waste, you use the same economy's you used in the past, even when you don't need to any more. You can be penny pinching and money grabbing, what you learn from periods of poverty, stays with you and sets you in good stead. The practical and material side of things always counts with you, you consider money. You don't loss your head. You will spend on some long awaited luxury, when you have a windfall, or have save enough for it, but your never foolish, you never put money on useless dreams, your not a waster, there is always a core of practicality with you and money. For you money equates with status. You like the self estimate a large sum gives you. Equally a blow to your bank balance can seem like a knock to your pride and your capability's.

You are one of the people who can make a small amount of money go a long way, and can live well on little if you have to There will be periods of poverty in your life, but you will also rise far above you beginnings and gain money and status. You are one of the signs that like to save or invest for your old age. In youth your financial position may be effected one way or another by your Father. And in the middle years you will gain great financial status. In money matters you are patient and persistent and you can wait for the time to ripen. You are shrewd and can often see opportunities for gain that others would miss and can even turn what seems a misfortune or loss into a gain. You avoid loss and claw back what you can in life. This way you keep a balance of things. You are cautious and can build up substantial assets.

AQUARIUS

This sign is favourable for money. You may have times of unstable erratic and uncertain finances in your life but these will also be punctuated colorfully with lucky streaks. You have a character that has substance and wisdom and can remain detached from money, so much so that other people wonder how you manage, how you make your living, when at times you seem to exist on nothing but air and behave independently as though you do not need money at all to live. You have values other than money and so you behave as though you don't need it. One of your aims or motives in having wealth or making money is to have freedom from the restrictions that poverty brings. You are generous to people who are more needy than yourself. You have a cautious and modest attitude to money, humanitarian, but never wasteful. You understand that only if you live well or free from want yourself can you then begin to do good in the world, or reach the higher visions of your mind and live up to your ideals.

Acquaintances and friends will greatly affect your wealth, and your finances are apt to swing from one extreme in life to the other, the caprices of fate, may be sensational. You like independence both financially and emotionally and may not like the mental burden of financial commitments, and debts, and of having others dependent on you, and so you keep things simple. You are generous with money and help and charity to strangers and causes, but you don't personally carry others if you can avoid it, you like people to pay their way, to be equal to share freely, you don't count the costs or who pays what but you are afraid of the commitment the restrictions that permanent dependents might make, afraid of the curtailment of the freedom to work at what you want or do without in the lean interludes and lavishness in the fat spells of life. Money is freedom from convention, commitment, from burdens in life that hold you back. But always you pursue your course unwaveringly, no matter how your finances fluctuate and always you have inner wealth, and inner belief in what you are trying to achieve.

There will be much uncertainty in your financial affairs, but you are adaptable to the winds of fate.

PISCES

Pisces has two rulers Neptune and Jupiter. When influenced by Neptune, it can and drain you and leave you only dreams instead of money, a desert where there used to be a rich seam,, and you can waste much money in self indulgence, pour it away for momentary pleasures that do not last but claw you back like a hook for more. With Neptune the value of money is to buy escape from the hardships and anxiety's of life. This is what you do with your money. You buy escape. Or if you learn the karmic lesson or Neptune correctly, Jupiter the other ruling planet of Pisces will take over and you can change your life. Turn everything around and begin to grow wealthy. The karma of Jupiter is to be creative in a practical successful way, to increase and build and extend what you have and make what talents you have, to have ambition and targets or goals. Jupiter also brings luck and lucky opportunities in life Taking a chance that pays off.

Jupiter makes you gain from and truly value other people generosity towards you and be sympathetic understanding and helpful to them in the process. To earn, to act, and be generous in a sensible way, not a wasteful way. Pisces is a sign that once it takes on a financial commitment carry's it's financial responsibility and burdens to the bitter end, you cannot put them down, no matter how you long to escape you trudge on financially. People depend on you, you are honest, supportive, and you pay your debts. you don't think of yourself as generous but you are. financially and otherwise. People take advantage.

Your finances will be very challenging and flowing. At times you are impractical and can loss money You long to make easy money and consequently can get caught up in schemes and faulted wisdom, promises that are supposed to make you wealthy but never do. Shady characters and dubious situations seem attracted like vultures to your weakness and gullibility and you ability to provide for others. You receive money from various sources some of which will be cloudy and obscure. This sign can attract wealth but has difficulty in hanging on to it for long. You waste, you weaken, and you are taken in by deceitful people and practices, by dead weights of dependents on your back. You are honest but not clear thinking, there is always some confusion in your financial situation, and you don't always see the way ahead, so that you make a decision that seem right and brings gain, but then as events unfold further it proves wrong or leads to losses in the end.

Sun sign astrology

The sign next to your zodiac sign will also tell you about money. In solar zodiac sign astrology the zodiac sign is the self, the equivalent of the first house in trued astrology, the sign next to your zodiac sign is the equivalent of your house of money. So that for example if your are born under Scorpio, you have a tendency to be secretive about your income and everything else in your personal life, but your solar house of money falls next door, in Sagittarius, a Jupiter ruled sign, so you will tend to be more wealthy in the second half of life than the first., because Jupiter improves things as time goes on. Zodiac sign astrology is scorned by many astrologers, because you can do it yourself without recourse to an astrologer, or other expensive expert. You don't need a personal consultation of your chart.

You need only the basics of knowledge, and while it is not totally accurate, it is a good beginning. Sit and think about the sign next to your own zodiac sign. What does it tell you about ways to increase your money? In our Scorpio example Sagittarius being the house after Scorpio, the equivalent of the second house, becomes the bank, Scorpios house of money. But. Scorpio becomes symbolic of the banks or 'moneys' twelfth house, or self undoing house. The house of self detriment. Scorpio is reserved, closed, shy and secretive. Sagittarius is more outgoing less inclined to brood on mistakes. Will being more outgoing, confident and optimistic help a Scorpio gain money or take the right risks? Will being less secretive allow him to get better advice? Jupiter is higher education. Is this Scorpio friend someone who has the brains and skills but hasn't bothered to follow up with the highest qualifications and training that could command a higher wage? Scorpio hides, Sagittarius puts itself forwards, is this what hinders? Sagittarius is religion politics, influence, beliefs and attitudes, do you have the wrong belief and attitude to make a lot of money, or to get on in life? Do you need to meet people of influence? If wealth is promise in the latter part of life, how can you speed it into the first half of life instead?

This is simple Sun sign astrology that anyone can do. Naturally only some things that become apparent to you while meditating on the next sign to yours apply to you, not everything. For there may be other aspects in your chart that contradict or nullify it.

Until your used to this basic form of zodiac sign astrology you may struggle, or be unable to make the zodiac sign fit at all Many a Scorpio sitting poverty will utterly fail to see how he can have wealthy Sagittarius influencing his money. Many a dreamy Pisces will totally fail to see how go getting Aries can possibly apply to him. Just as in our example, there will be things that do not apply to your Scorpio friend. But at least one thing will hit the target, one nugget of gold and truth will be found in the sand. Perhaps just a simple thing. The zodiac sign will always be stronger in it's influence than the money sign, so in our example Scorpio is going to be stronger than Sagittarius, this causes a blending of energy's, of meanings, the one dilutes the other like vodka and orange juice in a glass, it blends and alters and the orange changes, and is changed. Our Scorpio is secretive, our Sagittarius is a show off, and Sagittarius is all generosity. Therefore Scorpio is likely to show off his money but only in a discrete way, perhaps by his personal possessions, he won't brag but his shoes or bag may be expensive! He will be more generous to those he cares for than to himself but unlike Sagittarius not to all in sundry, and never openly. The one sign always modifies or melts the other in varying degrees.

The better you analyze simple zodiac sign astrology the more you can make of it. Taking basic zodiac methods a step further this way is an ample beginning to the arts of astrology. Using your own sign, then looking at your close friends, people you known well, so you can tell if your right or wrong, is a good way to learn, even if you consider yourself far beyond the basic stage of astrology, you can still enrich your learning by going back and revising this very basic technique. For most of the rest of the book we use more advanced or "proper" astrology.

Planets and signs in the 2nd house.

House Of Money

The second house of the horoscope is the house of loss and gain, it lies about thirty degrees beneath the ascendant in your chart and has a major influence over all financial affairs and monetary prospects. In the natal chart the star which rises on the cusp of this house and any planet positioned in it, or ruling this house will show you a fixed and certain fate. Depending on what that fate is, it is the future you have to either do all you can to encourage, so that goodness an riches blossoms greater in your life than is promised by the stars and the sacred money tree grows strong for you, or if it's a hard barren fate that's reflected there instead, you have to struggle all you can against it and overcome it. This is like making the Stony desert bloom with roses but the greater the challenge the greater the gain. The following paragraphs outline of the effect of the signs and planets in this house.

Moon

When the Moon is badly placed, weak or afflicted, it denotes debts, and a wastrel character, a dislike or shirking of responsibility's and immature attitudes to money; Fluctuations;, But when well placed or strong in the chart it can bring wealth. The Moon is also the area of the chart where one gets recognized, so the Moon can make or ruin your reputation. Wealth and fame are often coupled together like carriages on a train. In this house it gives you a financial reputation. Your money or debts get talked about. The Moon is the way you are seen by others to be, while the Sun is the way you are. So a second house Moon can give you the name of being the "rich one" in the family, the generous one, or it can make you known as the friend whose always cadging, begging and borrowing. The miser of the street; The one who's rich but looks poor and so on, the reputation or description it gives you depends on it's sign and strength.

Cancer

With cancer on the cusp of the second house, you have a psychological need for financial security, and an extremely cautious attitude towards anything connected with money and property. You have a tendency to horde money, a saver. Even when you are rich you find it had to shake off the insecurity or fear that a downturn may be just around the corner. And you plan accordingly. At times thrifty, at times generous, when your emotions are touched, like helping a member of your close family in their own times of poverty. You have strong sentimental feelings about heirlooms and ancestral possessions, and will tend not to sell things left to you, even if it is not financial viable to maintain them. Your background and your mother's attitude may have had an influence on you, You take out insurance policies, and may profit by them, money making ventures stand a good chance of succeeding for you.

Sun

You are money minded, but also wastefully extravagant, and if badly aspected poverty can be expected. The Sun in the second house is not always helpful to actual wealth, but it make can you look wealthy. It makes life more difficult and hard generally for the wealth is all on the surface. Pound rich penny foolish. Velvet curtains at the window, nothing in the house. Money is admired, wanted, the cost and the gain is thought of first in every situation Socially you measure people by their money, possessions, and standing. Mostly If you do a kindness you expect to profit. If you're generous you expect gratitude. You are both greedy and glamorous and money and what it can buy you or get you is everything to you. Financially with the Sun in this house you usually have quite a hard struggle to rise to wealth but it is always achieved in the end

Leo

You have the ability to work long and hard for money and with effort you can obtain quite a good income irrespective of whether you work for yourself of for others. At the same time you will have to watch expenditure for you will always have an urge to spend money and unless this is properly controlled you will over spend or find yourself taking up obligations and liability's that will not always be redeemed and will cause gaps in your income and embarrassment You are not necessarily personally extravagant but it will be extremely hard to refrain from spending money on showy luxury items.

Mercury

Loss or gain financially by learning, education or books. Tricky financial situations, where you will need to have an agile mentality. Slyness and shrewdness in monetary affairs. This placement can denote a person who is ingenious, full of financial wizardry, or equally on the negative shadow side, a cleverness turned to the bad, a swindler, pettifogger and fiddler, a chizzler who is full of thievery and cunning. Much depends on the sign and aspects made by Mercury in this house, if Neptune is in hard aspected to Mercury in this house, the person may find himself the victim of such thievery and fraud, rather than the perpetrator.

Gemini

You may enter into many complicated money-making schemes during your lifetime. The more you learn about money the better for your future. The less indecisive you will be. You will make your fortune more than once, but will loss it just as easily. The two sides of the twin are gain and loss. Too many choices present themselves to you financially. This sign tends not to be able to hold securely onto money once it has it. So part of the psychology behind the poverty you may endure might be to do more with not retaining the wealth, and with choosing the wrong path, missing the opportunity that was open to you. Something deep inside you wants not to hang onto the wealth.

Virgo

Virgo is the other sign Mercury rules. On the second house it means you are not dishonest but you are good at covering up your financial mistakes and miscalculations. You are realistic and cautious about money. Meticulous, mathematical, detail orientated, good at accounting, you read the small print of financial contracts and are carefull with investments. You are quite to criticize other peoples foolishness and their mishandling of their money, but slow to accept your own faults. Hard responsible work pays off for you. You run your financial affairs like clockwork, highly organised, practical, and efficient when it comes to managing your money, and equally good at handling other peoples money to their best advantage. You attend to bills and bank statements promptly.

Chiron

There may be a scar in the character to do with self worth that somehow reflects on the wealth or poverty. This planet also tells of financial injustices, and circumstance of loss beyond ones control that may be one ones fault but is hard to live with. Compensation and insurance settlements are likely to figure in your financial life more than most. Your financial affairs are in some way different or lacking something that others take for granted. The sign Chiron falls in can help show the wound that may be holding you back from making as much money as you could.

Taurus.

Money to you means security, material wealth, luxury, comfort independence, confidence. You have a realistic, practical and persevering attitude to money. A good business sense, you instinctively know the worth of things But you can be stubborn and cautious about taking risks. Dislikes following advice. You can prevent money coming to you by these things.

Venus

Generally fortunate in financial affairs. A love and desire for money. Opportunity. Sometimes a wealthy lover. Fortunate situations arise and there will be very little true hardship. Women influence your financial fortunes. Negative or dark side of Venus means you may suffer financially at the hand of a person or company who is reputed to be honest or has a good financial reputation and is well thought of, but for you is nothing but misery and loss. Bank mistakes, crashes and misfortunes of financial institutors and bank failures may also be a trouble.

Libra

You have a relaxed moderate attitude to money. Happiness or peace means more to you than wealth. There is at times a tendency to become financially dependent on others, becoming kept, or a burden on dependent on the good will and resources of those close to you. Your finances are affected by those of other people,. especially a partner, lover or family. There is also an inclination to burry you head in the sand and do nothing, when debts or poverty begins to over take you. The ability to sink into drudgery, working long hours and making do in poor circumstance for little profit if you are comfortable in your routine, or working for yourself in a labour of love but not really profiting. You want money and comfortable circumstance but you don't want the hard task of initiating it, or earning it, or being part of the rat race, if you can avoid doing so. You tend to endure or wait for someone else to step in and rescue you. Your lack of ruthlessness, and competitiveness can be your downfall financially. But this is also a sign that can be extremely successful. It brings popularity and other peoples support and resources.

Mars

Money may come and go quickly, waste, impatience and bad planning. Quarrels over money and disputes. Also you may have to fight for money or struggle to attain wealth generally in life. There is usualy an ambition to have money, or a desire to have " more" when Mars is in the second house, but it also means at certain times in life you may have to struggle to keep the money and wealth you have got, or fight to win what is rightfully yours in the first place., legal battles and competition over money.

Aries

You are kind hearted and charitable with money but may gain it by questionable methods, may waste much in the end. Money will drain away through unrealistic money making schemes, and get rich quick. Gambles. You want quick paths to wealth. But your karma may block this for along time. Though not forever. You will dream too much waste too much, poverty and debts will result. This can be countered. You will gain financial independence, self sufficiency, and then finally wealth.

Jupiter

Success and providence in money matters. Prosperity always comes, though this is not a planet of youth, usually it means money in maturity or the middle third of life. Money matters will also be associated with accolades status or honours that fall to you in life.

Sagittarius

You will be attracted to interests that involve making money, or the capitalization of your talents and inner ability's. Money will be drawn to you through these things without necessarily any voluntary action on your part. The use that you make of the opportunities that come will decide the degree of financial benefit you will ultimately derive. You have a strong liking for the luxuries and amenities of life but want money to come easily without undue effort. If this tendency is given way to there will be a danger of yielding to easy, or dubious temptations, speculations of ill repute that come into your life like driftwood on the tide brought by dubious circumstance, opportunities, or unscrupulous shady or immoral individuals who make clever suggestions, ideas, that whilst being attractive and cunning are not strictly honest or moral and if given into to could involve you in transactions of a fraudulent nature. Your main weakness is a reliance on others. But though this can aid you in obtaining money it will not bring permanent security. You don't think enough, you don't question enough. You need a wise partner or to cooperate with those who are strictly honest and straight forwards.

Saturn

Saturn is the planet of material limitations. Periods of poverty in life that may leave a permanent impression, or deep scars, but intermingled with the ability to rise. To pull yourself up by your bootlaces. A sense of purpose value and success. A character that is anxious about money, mean misery and saving. Rises the hard way in the great school of life. Has more wealth in later life than earlier life.

Capricorn

You have a steady and practical approach to earning money. You pride yourself on your self-discipline and wisdom. Capricorn on your second house is considered to be a money raking sign. It gives profit on investment. Whether the investment is money, or hard work. This house will bring you steady earnings which may be small at first but which will build up in time. At first you may be keenly aware of limitations financially and of lack of money. This may hamper your life. But the same sign will bring to you many opportunities that will pay off if you are prepared to put the long term effort in. This may be in work or in your own business or another job. In your own business conditions will be severe at the start. Because of your cautious character financially, you'll have good ideas but inadequate resources to set them in motion., or may not spend enough to get the business off the ground.

You will derive money and assist normal income as a result of proper planning and the courageous carrying out of plans into action. Many of your ideas will be practical, but you will need to be watchfull to see that others in higher positions do not usurp you and put the over their own ideas, thus denying you the right to rightful proceeds. The accepting of authoritative and responsible positions will aid the financial side of life, as a result of thrift you will be able to build up a substantial reserve. This sign is more favourable for investment than speculation, at times worrying conditions will arise as a result of delays or through you vocational

42

activity's being disrupted by national or international difficulty's, but your natural forethought will aid you in working through these periods.

Uranus.

Finances are in the capricious hands of fate, it foretells many changes and unsettled financial affairs. The tendency to reversals during ones lifetime. So that a person born poor with Uranus in their second house, may reverse his fortunes and end up rich. Or one born rich may fall on hard times. This planet means that you will learn to live with financial insecurity, and may even find it exciting. A lack of routines and stability but this need not be fearfull, Your financial life is like a wheel of fortune. Money will tend to flood in and then the opposite. A rich tapestry of dreams and reality. You may go from poor to rich and back many times in your life and be better for the experience of it. Even when you think you have learned all you can from this instability your finances are still apt to swing from one extreme to the other.

Aquarius

There is a detachment in monetary concerns, and money seems not to motivate you deeply, there are more important or valuable things than money, experience is one of them. You are less money orientated than most signs, but not foolish. This may be one reason why great wealth has not come. However you do value yourself and your work. Humanity and community and sharing resources, equality financially are all part of your attitude, you are less selfish than others, but you are unafraid to charge a fair price for what you do. If what you do is original or creative enough it can make you rich. For you have a kind of generous. You are practical and cautious financially, sometimes generous, sometimes mean, many contradictions in you. Acquaintances and friends, changing times, and large organizations will greatly affect your wealth.

Neptune

There is a danger of being lured into deceptive monetary dealings. Being robbed of money, so that it sinks away like rain into the soil, one moment there is a flood, the next it has all soaked away without your knowing. Or the reverse being the perpetrator of financial deceptions, frauds, shady dealings yourself It depends on signs and aspects. But usualy in the second house Neptune is the victim. This is a dependency sign, a parasitic sign, there may be periods when you do not earn your own money but live as a dependent off others, due to poor health, debts or poverty. There is a careless impractical approach to debts, and credit, unwise spending. Slip shod confused and approximate in dealings. You use your money to buy too many dreams. Addictions drain you of cash You live on hopes not reality. The positive side of Neptune is that money can be earned by some uncommon means, This planet makes for depression when financial matters don't work out. You are intuitive financially.

Pisces

You can gain money through creating good will. There may be seasonal fluctuations that can react on your work or business.

You could experience loss of money, through neglect and through lack of safeguards, or false friends, who act as a drain on you financially. Misplaced trust in things. When you have money you spend it. When you don't you have the illusion of wealth. You never look or act poor. There will be the inclination to make money easily or quickly but this will bring you into contact with dubious characters and so should be resisted.

Pluto

Long term transformation that will be extreme, the depths and the heights. Some sources of income will unexpectedly and suddenly stop, a new source will begin. Drastic but slow and total change.

Scorpio

Secrecy surrounds your financial matters. Even your main source of income may not be known to others. You tend not to keep your money all in one place. You may be secretive about your income, your saving, or you may have come from a background where talking openly about money, wages, cost of things, savings was not the done thing., Money and income was private, dark, taboo subject, kept to oneself. No one knew how the other one had. You run the risk of sinking dangerously into a state of debt, like a treacherous bog, that threatens to pull you under. Somehow you save and survive and usually have money salted away in different places.

Luna Nodes

Karmic debts that will be lived out through the money and
material affairs of life. The nodes usually bring a slow change of fortune, they turn the life and finances round as you work on your karma.

North Node

When you gain money, you will gain power or self confidence with it, karmic rewards, honesty in financial affairs. Some astrologers say the North node brings easy money, but I do not agree with this interpretation, because too often in people's charts I have seen an unwilling dependency on family or a partner, and a long struggle before the "easy money" comes. So many lessons have to learned first. Money, and lack of it, are the key to something vital with either node in this house.

South Node

The person may waste or squander the wealth the substance they have consequently fortunes may dwindle. Perpetual waste. The person may be deceptive and dishonest, or tricky and unfair in financial situations. Sometimes the South Node brings money from inheritances, or the efforts of the past.

Many Planets

Many planets in the second house mean great desire for money, but generally an equally great paucity or lack of it! ; Two or three badly aspected or ill dignified, forewarn of great poverty. Good aspects mean good opportunities in life but usualy carrying with them a fate, or a price that may not emerge until much later. An example would be mixed good and hard aspects that linked the seventh and second house, such a fate might be to marry money but for that marriage to be unhappy or too high a price to have paid for the wealth. Links between the house of money and health that were bad, may also mean sacrificing ones health for gain, as many people down the century's in heavy industry have, the coal miners coughing up black dust and destroying their lungs, the radiated power station workers. Money got through compensation for works injuries. The chart would warn of the possible fate, it gives a choice. If you read the complex aspects and links in your chart correctly, you can get all the details. But given this foresight would you at the time when you are wrapped so tightly in the tangle of emotions and hopes, with the blindfold of every day circumstance around you, be able to see your way ahead?, Would you be strong enough to resist the lure of the stars? Or would you walk into the trap. The stars can advise, they can warn, but they cannot compel, we make our own decision. Character is everything. If you want both money and a good life it's important to have strength of character. Multiple good aspects from or to, Uranus, Saturn, Mars, have the possibility to be able to change your financial circumstance from evil to good. Multiple bad aspect, the reverse, a fall and loss of finances in life, unless great care is taken.

Influence of Transits to Second House

The transits in the chart are important in determining what will happen in the future. An astrological chart or natal chart as it is called, is like a picture of the stars as if they were at birth frozen in time at your birth, They reflect a basic fate, the karma you are given at birth. But as the positions of the stars change over the years and days after your birth, a transit is a way of showing how far the stars and planets have moved since then and what that effect has. A transit causing things to surface form the original natal chart, it empowers various planets and makes them active, when they may have been dormant before and it adds it's own influence to the chart as it passes, it trails it's own medley of events and happenings into our lives. An event or a possibility lies sleeping in a chart until a transit causes it to wake and happen. When it does it may bring joy or havoc Transits being temporary, pass again. They are so not fated, in the essential way as natal planets are. In a many chart a transit cant brings a run of good, so we must take advantage of it while it's there Transits are all important in predicting future wealth, and in advising what to invest in and when, A good transit can show the most opportune time to invest in something, to sell something, to take a risk,. A bad transit can show when to stop investing in a thing, when to cut loose, before the shares plummet. A good transit can make us richer, a bad one can help us prevent misfortune. Transits help us win at life.

If you can chart read but haven't learned transits yet, now is the time to begin !. It will add a whole new dimension and interest to your astrology. Have a printed copy of your chart wheel on your table. Then all you have to do is find out the position of the planets today, or next week or next year, this doesn't involve any complex maths, though you can work it out mathematically if you want, and if you'd lived a couple of hundred years ago, it would have been the grim and only way of doing it! Today you can find out where the transits are from astrological sites on the internet, or from using a book of Ephemeris, which lists in collums, the positions of all the planets for each day of the year, and for years and years ahead.

Begin the simple way first. Look to see what sign Jupiter is in during the month of year of the future that you want to know about. Don't trouble about the degrees and details just yet. If you're using a book of ephemeris the symbol of the planet is at the top of the collums. Below the symbol is a list of numbers, and there is the symbol for the sign the planet is in. Suppose Jupiter is in Leo. Look to your own chart and see where Leo is. If you have Leo in your third house, then *Jupiter is transiting your third house.* Look to the sign Saturn is in, suppose he is in Aries, look to see which house Aries occupies in your chart. Maybe it's in the eleventh house, then we say *Saturn is transiting your eleventh house.*

When you are familiar with finding where a transit planet is placed in your chart. Then check the exact degree of sign of the transiting planet. The degree he is transiting through is listed in the collums of numbers below the planets symbol. Some planets move slowly, hardly a degree a month, others may move several degrees in a month. Pluto for example may have the same degree all month. So suppose in the Column under the Pluto symbol, you see the sign for Capricorn. You know that Pluto is transiting through Capricorn. Then the list of numbers in the Column, goes 13. 20. 1. then below it 13. 21. 0, then below that 13. 20. 9. all the way down the Column, three numbers. It is only the first number we are interested in. It means *Pluto is thirteen degrees into Capricorn.* If the first number right down the Column is 13, it means *Pluto is thirteen degrees into Capricorn all month.* The other two numbers in the Column are or fractions of a degree. If the first degree were to change from 13, to 14, it would mean Pluto had moved a degree further into Capricorn that month. Some planets transit through several degrees in the space of a month.

If you're using the Ephemeris, you use it like a graph. The day and month of each year are in the first Column,. The planets along the top, so you can read the exact position of the planet for any day of the month.

Now that you know the exact degree and sign a planet is transiting, you can look again at his exact position in your chart and correct it if necessary. This is where transits get just a little bit more complicated and confusing for the beginner. If Jupiter was transiting at twenty degrees into Gemini, and the ninth degree of Gemini was the degree and sign on your eleventh house cusp, then as before Jupiter would be transiting through your eleventh house. But if Jupiter was transiting at three degrees into Gemini, he wouldn't have yet reached the cusp of your eleventh house, he would be still be in your tenth house. It's a small detail but it's an important one. He wouldn't have crossed into your eleventh house yet,. The sign on your house cusp is like a door step, it has some of it's degrees, outside of the door, and some inside of the door. The easiest way to remind yourself which side is which, when working out where the transit is in your chart, is to Think of the transiting planets as someone, an old mythic god walking anticlockwise round the houses,. He knocks at each house door in the circle of stars, enters and as he passes through, he brings his gifts with him.

There is one exception. The transit Luna node, which is not a planet but a point. She travels clockwise round the circle!.

When I was learning astrology, in the books of all the Great old astrologers, who I admired and still do admire, would give complex and quasi-scientific baffling explanations of how the universe worked astronomically the transit planets went anticlockwise in the chart. Why the east and west horizons seemed transposed. These ancient astrologers used mysterious technical phrases and words like. " The plane of the celestial equator" and "Oblique ascension". "The meridian" It made a simple task into something complex, One could read it and still not know why astrology was "back to front", with it's eastern horizon where the west would be. As far as I in my ignorance at that age was concerned, it was an occult art, so everything in reverse is natural. I did not even question it. I did not need to understand it scientifically and it took a long struggle for me, an uneducated person to do so. This is why when I'm explaining things to you, I put myself back in the beginner's boots. I perhaps over simplify them and under-technify them, because it is easer to grasp this way. You can acquaint yourself with the Jargon and more exact science of it all later. I am of the cavalier attitude that one doesn't need know how or why the vacuum cleaner works in order to clean the floor. A little knowledge helps, too much confuses.

There is joy in modern day because the computer will work out the transits and chart and anything else for you, but it is still good to have a rudimental knowledge of how it works, just as a car driver doesn't need to know the detail of how the robots made her car, but a basic knowledge of how it should work may her re start the car if the engine fails, or help her to know when the thing just isn't going quite right.

Without astrology and the great astrologers of old there would have been no astronomy. Astronomy is scientific while astrology is symbolic. They are like mother and daughter, quite separate entity's which bare a vague ancestral resemblance to each other but are not the same, and shouldn't be expected to be.

Coming back to transits for those who are beginners. Once you are familiar with which house in your chart and which degree the transit is in, you can then proceed to get a little bolder. The transiting planets make aspects to your own planets,, transiting Jupiter in your tenth house, will eventually make a conjunction to any planet you had in that house when you were born. As he makes his way round the chart he makes other aspects just as the planet in your birth chart make aspects to each other. When your first learning concentrate on learning one aspect at a time, the conjunction, then the squares, and then the opposition, leave learning the other aspects the transit makes until you are more proficient. Learn step by step, don't attempt to learn everything at once. When I was a small child my Father taught me to play chess, on an antique chess set, he'd brought home from a sea voyage with wonderful carved fascinating figures. I learned one piece at a time. Only the pawns at first, like a game of checkers. Then we added the knight, or Queen. When I became thoroughly conversant with the way each piece moved, what it was called and what the game meant we added another piece or rule to each game. This is the way I teach you, little by little in each book I write for you, and one day you will know all I know, and hopefully more than I will ever know, because you will research, and observe, and will work more things out yourself.

Planets that happen to be crossing or aspecting the second house, or the eighth house of the sky at any given time bring with them the winds of financial change. They conjure up events that are transient, temporary, not permanent they blow in like the fallen leaves to our door, but they can still have far reaching effects. Pluto for example can take ten years to move through sign, so if he begins to aspect your house of money his effects are enduring. While the suns transit will lasts only about month. Here is some astrological observations and advice that may help you manage your money better in keeping with the passage of the transits through your chart.

In General, do not make investments when a planet transiting your house of money, or the planet ruling it has turned retrograde. A retrograde planet loses something of it's power, the result can be at best a poor return for your money, at worse a complete financial reversal and loss of money invested instead of a gain.

When the ruling planet of the second house is retrograde by transit, there is danger of loss of money or the taking on of debts. A danger that anything bought will be substandard or disappointing, that you may have to take it back to the shop, or any contract entered into financially will be regretted. Therefore it is wise to avoid such transactions at that time. To improve the astrological influence at such times it is good under retrograde influences to take action to pursue people who owe you money, of action for the return or refund of goods and moneys, as the retrograde can work in your favour and draw things back that you have previously paid, given up or lost. To cash things in, claim a refund on a ticket, to look for lost items, to find money in the pockets of coats you haven't worn for a long time and so on. This is a simple example of working with that astrology of your chart rather than against it, if you do this all the time, you will improve your financial fate and maximize your wealth, first in small trifling ways then in bigger ones, to do so attunes you to your potential, all things escalate and accumulate. Opening up a celestial hatch of potential, is like opening a bottle of wine, first a trickle then a glassful, then a bottle, then a crate.

Transits from Uranus, if Uranus is powerfull, it means your wealth and substance will change from bad to good. But When transit Uranus is weak it means it will go from good to bad. The same can be said of Saturn and Mars transits. The Moon's progression through the second house, or it's transits when unafflicted makes for wealth, or gains, but if weak enfeebled or afflicted brings poverty or losses instead. South Node transits indicate money will be wasted. North node; lessons will be learned.

The ruling planet of the second house when afflicted by a baleful planet or malevolent aspect, or enfeebled by being retrograde, always warns you against loaning money to others and against borrowing it yourself, as it will not be paid back, or only recouped with the greatest of struggles.

When the ruling planet of the tenth house, or the planet occupying the tenth house and acting as ruler, crosses through the second by transit, this is usualy fortunate and there will generally be a financial increase and subsequent rise in status. A better wage or a better job. The slower moving the transit the greater the increases and change in financial matters. But with planets like Pluto and Saturn, and other signs of change, an old source of income may have to terminate first before the new and more profitable one begins, and the period of ending and dwindling resources may cause temporary struggle or despair. The Career itself (tenth house is house of career) is often not changed, but financial aspects of it are.

When the ruling planet of the second house transits the tenth there is money to be made through career or investments and people connected with the career. The Career itself is sometimes also changed during this transit. Working for a firm for more money, or the gaining of a better paid job.

When Saturn is in aspect to the Sun or Moon, there is often delay, and if he is retrograde a bigger delay, so that even when the chart looks fortunate financially, the wealth may not come untill obstacles have been removed, or if it a life time reading, untill later in life.

Mum and Dad's Pockets

In astrology the father is represented by the Sun. An afflicted Sun suggests the father was a poor man, miserly or of not much help to you financially. He may have lacked opportunities himself and been unable or unwilling to help advance his children's future. He may have been absent or died early. Or taken no interest in the child's financial experiences of poverty or wealth, what was spent on him, what was not, his pocket money, allowance, and so on, it may have been left to the mother.

The Moon is a mother symbol, and the same applies to an afflicted Moon. If the Moon is afflicted by Saturn (the affliction or Moon being aspected to, or in the house of money, or fourth house, the childhood was made poor by the mother. The fourth is the house of childhood, The mother may be economic, self denying, miserly, regardless of income, she may horde money only the bare essential of it utilized, the rest stashed away. While if the Moon is afflicted by Neptune, and influencing the houses of money. The mother may be poor because of wistfulness, squandering, gambling drugs or drink, or by supporting someone unworthy, or in poor health. If Jupiter afflicts, she will impress others with money while keeping her own children short. An afflicting Uranus, and she is not maternal with money, she is not mean but the priority is her own life, it goes on other things.

If both the Sun and Moon share the afflictions, then neither mother nor father were able to give the child much of a financial life and the scars of that are likely to follow the child into adult life and perpetuate some kind of continuing poverty.

If the aspects in the chart are not malefic to or afflictions, but instead are good aspects, then regardless of the parents personal income, money would have been bestowed on you and your childhood experience and memory of it would have been one of wellbeing. It may have been experienced as abundant or even if you noticed poverty in the home, you will not have suffered by it, but been given pocket money and treats, and your childhood as much as possible made the same as others you knew.

In your own individual chart, the ruler of the tenth house and fourth house, represents the parents Along with the Sun and Moon. Usually the tenth is the father, and the fourth the mother, but in some charts it can be the reverse. These chart formations will tell you about the influence money had in your childhood. Self analysis of that basic pattern, will tell you about basic subconscious beliefs that have grown out of that, if the pattern was good then your beliefs and ability to gain money in later life will be easier, but if bad then until you correct the belief you cannot alter the pattern of the future. Let's look at some other childhood patterns in the next section of the book.

Fragments Of Childhood

There is a psychological link between money and emotion. There is the person who try's to buy love and friendship, with generosity, gifts and money. (additional Chart aspects to look for are ruler of the eleventh, seventh or fifth house, in hard aspect to ruler of the house of money or Jupiter.) Issues of self worth, need to be tackled. Fears of rejection, or of not doing well enough, The inner voice of the subconscious says "they won't love me if I have nothing to give them". The older root of this is in a childhood where you're made to feel cast aside, or of small importance, not loved quite enough, untill you behave as the parent demanded. A childhood where you had to "purchase" love, by being good, or by "giving" the parent what they expected, and were left to feel alone and emotionally abandon, devoid of loving, unlovable if you didn't comply. The experience would have been reinforced through out life in many subsequent relationships. Like night follows day, your willingness to "give" in exchange for love, would attract people with a willingness to take. So the early forgotten pattern repeats and worsens because the only way to stop the walk away is to give more. There is endless supply of people who can be bought. Untill you overcome this old psychological pattern, friendships, relationships, other people will always be a drain on your income.

If you are one of those people who use money to buy friendship and love in a similar but more conscious way, using. money as power to manipulate and buy others. It can come from a childhood where you parents bribed you, bought your silence, or your good behaviour. A bar of chocolate to stuff in your mouth and keep you quiet while Mum shopped. A new toy, if you were good, to show off to your friends and make you superior. If you pass the exam, something nice promised to you, and so on. Money was power and status in some way, commodity to be traded, and you've never forgotten it. Now in adult years, like the first example, you buy people, but you don't fear rejection, because your parents never rejected you, neither did they teach you what real love means. They "employed" you to be good, and unconsciously taught you how to employ and bribe other people. The people and things who will hurt you are always the ones who cannot be bought, the ones who you will long for but cannot have. The ones who show no interest in you. If this is a theme in your life issues about self importance seniority, and lack of it, need to be worked on before there can be real happiness in your character and power and gain in life.

When we work one level of life, for example our character or early conditioning and make changes in outlook we work on all the other layers of life simultaneously. All things are connected spiritually. Sometimes it is not possible to work directly or materially on increasing our money, but at such times we can still work psychologically on detecting the reasons for our lack of money and on removing those old impediments.

Then there is the ragged child of a poor family whose is made to feel money is far too precious to waste on him. He may turn into an adult who feels guilty when given a gift that he has not reciprocated or when he buys a new car or expensive jacket. The housewife who buys the dress, hides it in the drawer and tells her husband it was much cheaper, or a gift from her sister. The person who wont spend her own money on things she needs or loves, and when she does buy, always buys the cut price bargain instead of the costly item she really desires, even when she has more than ample cash in her purse. All these scenarios have psychological links with the past, occasionaly with past marriages or relationships but usualy with childhood too.

If this kind of pattern is subtly destroying your chances of prosperity (there will most likely be Saturn Moon aspects that connect with Jupiter or with the ruler of the money houses). To remedy it you need to make your deeper self know that what may have been appropriate in childhood, because of parental hardship or meanness or attitudes to wastage is not appropriate now, even if condition haven't changed much the big change is that YOU are in charge of your own life now. And this ancient pattern and everything based on it and has been built up around it must be discontinued if wealth is to grow.

In a childhood of miserliness and denial, where everything is saved nothing spent, the child may grow to continue the pattern of hoarding money but denying himself things he could buy, The person who has thousands in the bank but scuffed holed shoes on his feet. Or he may rebel psychologically and go the opposite and waste lavishly, as if trying to fill himself with the sweets and treats he did not get in childhood compensate himself for past hardships. Either extreme is not conducive to wealth, and the psychological blockage to be worked on is to leave the past influence behind. To find a sensible balance between saving and spending. It is interesting that Saturn, who often determines a chronic life long frugality when conjunct the ascendant or Sun, is also the planet of the past. When Saturn makes any aspects to the Moon the frugality is more one of self denial and often learn in the formative years by unconscious example from a parent who may also be self denying, guilty, hording and saving, with the Moon aspects there is the illusion that there is not enough money. This may be true of both childhood and adult years. With the Sun aspects there is genuinely not enough money in childhood and the child is kept poor. But both are impediments from the past that have to be unlearned for the future to change.

In each fragment of childhood described through out this book, there is a history where the child picks up the psychological message that money is considered more valuable than the child, the person. Material and emotional survival, go hand in hand but in infancy when a child is less able to differentiate subtly between love and emotional and material survival this self value, of being worth less than money, not worth the money spent on him, or that money spent on him was wasted, wasn't his right had to be earned and so on, may have become amalgamated into one thought entity in the subconscious mind. If we can undo the damage of the past thought, the future self is free to heal from the old scars and become and wealthier. Before anything can be undone it has to be recognised. Recognition of what has been done to you is the firsts step in healing.

Try to Identify the childhood pattern in your own chart. It may be one of the patterns in this book, or it may be something else altogether, for this book is not comprehensive, it is only an outline of psychological possibility's, that is intended to make you think for yourself and inspire you it will not give all the individual answers Only you are you, and you are unique. When you find your pattern, then try to analyze and alter it, by finding the right kind of self worth and self importance, and by breaking past physiological links, and patterns you will remove the blockages that lead to self imposed poverty. This will leave money free to flow like a wonderfull river into your life.

The Tragedy Of Poverty.

South Node

Wherever the South Node falls in a chart it shows the cause of loss of poverty in ones life. Their bad influence spoils your chance of success and wealth They destroy future opportunities which are on the horizon, so that ill luck appears to continue or poverty to blight your life when it need not. By reading the South Node, you find what you have to correct in your life, karma or thinking, in order to stop the ongoing loss and help gain wealth.

In the First

The person brings his own ruination or downfall in some way. He is his own worst enemy in making money.

In the Second

He is poor through circumstance outside his control.

In the Third

For example, the education may have been poor, or lacking, or the person has not gained the qualification that would advance him, or he may be some hindrance to learning that he must overcome, or find a way around.

In the Fourth

The background may have hindered wealth, and encourage poverty. Also loss through property, rents mortgages. You need to correct emotionally or material dependency on others.

In the Fifth

Gambling risk taking, may have caused losses, the children may have been a source of poverty

In the Sixth

Health or lack of it has influences the income or ability to make money. People employed to work for you or do things for you, underlings. Life's events have not served you instead they have contributed you poverty, paying to much for jobs to be done, goods supplied and so on.

In the Seventh

Marrying or close love relationship, divorces, mistress, lovers, the opposite sex, have contributed to your poverty. Either the partner's income, inheritance or ancestry, the eventual death or the partner that may leave you unprovided for, or absence of others at various times in life who would have helped you become wealthy. Poverty by struggling to much alone. Also the legacy of marriage, dowry or partners wealth is destroyed or absent or too meagre and adds to the poverty.

In the Ninth

He may be helped by the higher mind, religious institutions, spiritual studys. Or made poor by them.

In the Tenth

the career or calling has made you poor. Or lack of it

In the Eleventh

Friends have kept you in poverty and stopped you gaining more or being more ambitious.

In the Twelfth

You are poor through karmic difficulty, and adverse circumstance. The working of enemies' curses.

The transit South Node is symbolic of the past being brought to bear on the future, or present time. It can bring karmic misfortune, losses that are not your fault, but conspire around you like malevolent circumstance, and may have karmic origins in a previous life. In a past life it may have been your fault. But either way transit node time is come upance time., and if it is in a part of the horoscope to do with money, for example conjunct the ruler of the house of money, the come upance is connected with money. Very occasionaly it can bring the reverse, karmic rewards, an unlooked for sum.

Healing after Theft

The Loss

A loss of money by theft can leave a sickness of the spirit, a wound like any other loss. Like any other scar this can impede your progress in life. Do not let a thief leave his leprous hand on your spirit. If someone steals from you be it money, or your ideas, your work, or some other things of value, and uses that thing to their own profit. and consequently to your loss. If they steal your name or reputation. Your staff, your customers, your business, your livelihood from you. Whatever is stolen, unless you allow it to hurt or anger you, or to embed it's carnivorous teeth in your soul, they have taken nothing of the essential you, nothing of true value. Nothing you cannot replace.

A Thief in Your Life

Do not allow the intrusion of a thief into your life to damage or taint you with their own pernicious evil, to do so is to allow them a further victory. A neighbour lived in a rooming house near me, she was burgled by people who persuaded her landlord that they were her close relatives come to visit her, so he let them into her room in her absence. They took money, but worse, her precious photographs from long ago, years back, and mementoes, gifts, treasured cherished things, irreplaceable things, things of memory were taken from her, some destroyed in the ransacking for no reason at all. Two years on, she told me

"I never used to hate people, I worked as a nurse looking after people. I never hated anyone, but now I do. I'm not the woman I was and never can be again. My neighbour moved to a different town, she no longer felt safe in her own room, and it was stained, besmirched by the memory".

She had previously loved the street, having arrived as an immigrant and virtually homeless, she had built up her life there, her job, her home, and her friends. Now it was all destroyed Two years on from the theft we met in the town centre by pure chance and she still carried the trauma of the incident in her spirit. It is as though the thief had not only taken something irrevocably, that cannot be returned but had left something dark and cancerous instead it's place. Some people recover from theft, others are left with a fear, mistrust, a hate, a sickness of the soul that will not ever go away. Depression too is a common aftermath.

Losing your Lifestyle

All things, possessions, money, intelectual or physical property, identity, reputation are an extension of the self, so sometimes when things are taken the self is damaged by it, they have taken away and damaged a part of your essential self, be it your security your feeling of strength and self power. The ability to protect yourself is taken, or scratched at the very least. The feeling of safety in your own home is gone, you're trust, or your faith in the goodness of humanity. In some cases, like my neighbour more precious inner things are irreparably lost, good memorys, a good home. The subtle loss of a lifestyle. Never again will she or I enjoy the simple pleasure of chatting to each other over my garden gate on a summer's day. That small part of her life, along with everything else unnoticed but valued has been thieved too, countless other small things that were part of her former life here in this street, in her room. The pattern the Sun light made on her wall, the sound of the town hall clock chiming or the cry of the sea birds, the salt smell of the tides. And the entire thing she moved away from. They are gone, small things, insignificant but they are gone. The damage of theft can spread wider than that event, like poison in a pond for the victim, it pollutes everything around it on so many levels.

Losing your Spirit

Do not allow robbers and thieves, muggers, this extra power. They have already taken something material, don't let them take from you spiritually or emotionally as well, for that can be the greater wound. The reaction of many people whose house has been burgled for the first time, is to move away, they no longer feel safe there. But once is too soon if it's a home you have loved, you need to give your home a second chance. If your home becomes a repeated target for burglary hatred and vandalism moving may be the only thing to do to end it. But if so, do not look on the solution as defeatist. You can make any house into a lovely house, but you cannot change the place it is in, or make a bad street into a good one. Look on it as a move towards better quality of life and wealth, a future gain. But also acknowledge that to do so means the burglar has stolen your home away, your happiness, and taken part of your life from you, parts you did not want to give. The small pieces as well have been taken like change from your pocket. Everything and everyone you knew, and enjoyed there, from the corner shop where you'd buy that forgotten loaf of bread, to the song of the bird on your back wall. To the old lady, on the corner whose day you'd cheer up by saying say Hello to, or the kid three doors down who proudly showed you her new doll. All gone. Every domestic thief is a stealer of lives.

Kings of Thieves

In the chart, Neptune and Mercury are the planetary Kings of Thieves generally. Their place in the radix chart, shows where you are most likely to suffer from theft. The transits show the imminent threats from theft, including from con merchants, burglars, salesmen, treacherous schemes, friends and relatives and anyone who will misappropriates your money. If you have Neptune in the radix twelfth house for example, you are more likely to suffer theft by treacherous behaviour or the sneak thief. The "hidden enemy". And subtle thefts, while in the second the theft will be directly money.

When Neptune transits the fourth or aspects it's cusp, beware of bent property deals, theft from your house. Theft of your house.

Violent theft

This is a bigger issue, with its own trauma and own astrological aspects, it will involve Mars, plant of aggression attacks, and fighting and sometimes Pluto, as well as Neptune or Mercury. The eighth and twelfth house, are often involved

More than Money

Theft isn't always money, some things have a different value. I have Neptune in my twelfth house. Some years ago a well known professional Occult person, consulted me on a number of occasions for an astrology reading for herself. She stole a paragraph from my work. For all I know she may have stolen several such paragraphs. It was an explanatory rather decorative piece of text, Neptune creates mystery's for which there are sometimes no explanations. Why didn't she write her own paragraph? The text was hardly a wonderful work of art that couldn't be reproduced. She began to put this one paragraph in all her own clients' readings. Sometimes there are only a fixed number of variations on how the same thing can be said. Theft of words can be unintentional or accidental. Words find their way into the subconscious and they may come out again unaltered, we may think them our own but someone else may have said them or written them first, but not this, it was an exact "paste and copy" job, right down to my misspellings and casual grammar, I was mystified.

If she had asked me if she could have it I would have happily given her it I would have even been flattered that she wanted it and simply written myself different paragraph, our friendship would have blossomed by it, but instead her deception tarnished the bond and though I said nothing for it was a trivial thing I could not think of her again in the same way. Not for a long, long time. Untill I later found what a difficult patch she had been going through in her own life. The theft only came to light when one of her clients who wanted a second opinion of her unhappy fate sent me a copy of the Occultist reading. The great thing with Neptune in the twelfth house, the theft can be hidden from view for a long time, the twelfth house is the house of concealment, but eventually it will always be found out. Neptune is the depth of the ocean, where things can be lost for century's, including lost truths like sunken ships but where and all things surface in time.

Forgiveness

The positive side of Neptune is forgiveness and transcendence. If you forgive someone it is healing, it removes the thorns from your flesh, but it's not something you can choose, it's alchemy deep in the heart that either happens or it doesn't. Sometimes you have to work very hard to make it happen Some people find it easier to forgive than others, Don't ever blame yourself if you cannot forgive. Feeling you should forgive someone, when you can't, when you simply don't have it in you, adds needlessly to your own pain and guilt when the fault was never yours.

Forgiveness is important, but not for any of the reasons we are taught to believe. Theft is a thorn that leaves splinters in the soul, we have to root them out one by one so that they heal instead of fester on. Forgiveness is for you, for your own benefit, it removes scars, it helps the healing process. Forgiveness is not for the thief's benefit. A thief can only benefit form learning better, from lessons in the hard school of life not from being forgiven. It can be galling to see an evil person prosper in our place, or gain from what they have taken from us, or go unpunished. But what is gained financially is one part of life, if it's gained unfairly or wrongfully, there is usually corresponding loss in another part of life.

Forgiveness is not about helping the thief's soul. What happens to that person doesn't matter. Destiny will deal with them as she sees fit. It is not your concern. Forgiveness is not about forgetting, it's not about becoming a holier or better, or good person. It's not about forsaking revenge, or setting aside justice and allowing injustice to prevail in your life. It's about closure, about caring less for those who are against you and caring more for yourself. Forgiveness is about self healing, it removes the thorns of anger and bitterness from the flesh, the fearfulness or mistrust or great disappointment felt, the event is no longer important or unsettling, it can be left behind. It removes the power the other person has had, like a splinter from your flesh and gives that power back to you. The flesh is healed and renewed without scar. Those who can forgive find it brings closure. It means every last thing is dealt with, every last poison is able to be drained from the pond so it no longer pollutes the soul.

The Worst Kind

The worst kinds of thieves are those who are known to you. They steal more than money or items, they steal your trust and self worth. Families are riddled with sneak thieves. You open up a family, you find a worm in the apple. The child who steals a few coins from its mother's purse, it goes unnoticed till it becomes a habit. The older son who systematically but sneakily robs his siblings or his parents cash box to squander the money on drugs, or gambling. The student son whose family always bails him out of the debts he runs up. Mothers go into denial they make excuses for their children, they cover up. I have known a young boy steal from his father and the mother put the money back before the boy was found out and punished. She feared the fathers rage and wanted to protect the boy. The boy lived with the father's anger and mother protection every day. If the mother had clear insight she would have realized the boys continued thieving spelled a lack of respect for her and abuse of her protection, and that could only become worse in adult life. Children don't learn without being taught.

Parents blame the "bad crowd" the child is mixing with at school, or that he " Takes after" someone, or that he is not right in the head. Or that they must be mistaken, that it is not him, the money was miscounted, or taken by someone else. Or that they shouldn't have refused to loan him money, then he wouldn't have had to steel. That the child is a child and hasn't learned better yet. The true fact is all children are taught in infancy, what belongs to them and what doesn't., which toy belongs to the friend, or the sister, which item they can touch, which they cannot because it is not theirs to touch. What to give back, what to put down. Its leaned by the age of three.

A client's relative by marriage stole a month's money from her purse,. "At the time I had neither the money nor success I have now. I probably had less than her, " the client said, "she knew I had nothing but stole it anyway. " There was no mitigating circumstance at all, not one crumb. With the money she took away trust and generosity and left behind a profound depression. My client's kindness she curdled into sour milk, the relative had been staying at my client's house. My client was left to ask, was she so unvalued in herself, that relative of her husband whom she had from inner goodness, or kindness allowed to stay at her home, at her expense, had stole from her? Was she so worthless to her husband's family that her feelings, her thoughts, her difficulties that ensued from this clandestine theft did not matter at all? This is part of the power of relatives, they do things in silence, it can become "our little secret" like an abuse that we are locked into without choice, so as not to disturb the others in the family, or because we know the perpetrator is the one more valued to he family than us., Our lives are complex and concessionary when it comes to relatives, step relatives and in laws. Our lives are not always under our own choice.

The Victim

Every victim walks a different road, for some it's paved with anger, and cemented with rage. For some it's dispisement, for other fear and powerlessness but for each the road is an inner one. The client treated the relative no differently outwardly for the situation was complicated. If blood ties in familys are a seething can of worms, then marriage familys, and step familys are twice the can, for there is often the additional slap in the face that the marriage partner, like the deluded mother who will not see her own child for the thief he is, will not take your part and in so doing devalues you even more and sides subtly with the wrong doer, the thief. Old ties are stronger than new, blood is thicker than water. They will explain it away, make excuses,. They accuse you of miscounting, over spending, getting it wrong, you must be mistaken because the "Holy family" of in laws or steps, are the great trinity who can never be wrong. They are enshrined forever, faultless like the saints. So you end up your trust betrayed by both by the thief and the partner. Those who should love you best, love you worst, ripples in a pond. The road made lonelier.

Disloyalty to you is another way you walk alone. That once the reflection is shattered is never again the same, even if it outwardly pretends to be, truth is lost, communication clouded. The ties of blood stain the water and nothing is ever reclaimed. It's always more than money that is taken from you. You can sometimes get money back, but not the other things.

Other Aspects

Along with Neptune and Mercury that are the planets of thieving hands (Mercury symbolise the hand and the pen. Neptune the sleight of hand, the fraudulent signature) Chiron and Jupiter are sometimes involved in misappropriation of money and theft. Chiron because he rules unfairness. These planets in the third and twelfth house in aspect to each other, represent deception by your siblings or close neighbours, or the friends of your children. If they are ninth and twelfth your partners siblings, your college friends, your step- children's friends, Uncles and Aunts. The eleventh house symbolises your step-children, and your friends or acquaintances. The fifth your own children. The fourth house represents your own home. There is a whole art to identifying a thief, astrologically but these clues more serve to forewarn you of the areas of your life where you may be vulnerable, so you can take action to prevent theft and loss. An antidote to this kind of theft, is the old saying Success is the best revenge, especially if you can flaunt in their face!

More upsetting than the family thief or "in house" thief, is the faceless, shadowy, sly undercover thief. This is when for instance, money is taken, or some other valuable or treasured thing, and you know from the circumstance of the theft it could only have been taken by one of say a dozen people. These twelve were all your trusted valued friends. Now everything becomes tainted, it is no one and everyone now, they are all suspects. They all cleave your heart like raw meat that begins to turn rotten.

Is it this beloved friend who embraces you so sweetly to say goodnight, is her kiss the Judas kiss. ? A thief is a suffocator of souls, a despoiler of friendships. Is this boy who you raised like your own son the dishonest one, has he waited his rat like chance, knowing the blame would fall on someone else? Does the one who chats so pleasantly to you despise you enough to steal from you? Someone has. Someone thinks so little of you, while seeming to think so much. Can you trust your lover, your partner ? And so it goes on the slime like strands of suspicions we weave from not knowing, a garment of repulsion that only truth can free us from and everything becomes like spoiled fruit, crushed lily's, for who ever did steal the item has damaged all of you in the circle. There is a wall or mistrust and uncertainty between you and friends where previously there was none. And sometimes many years on it becomes the first crevice in a crumbling wall of abandonment and ruins of past friendships are all that remain in years to come. There is nothing, at the time you may not imagine the incident struck at the foundations of the circle.

So long as there is a thief in your life there is a deterrent to wealth. As long as there is the aftermath of theft, there is a still a thief in your life.

Remedies

How to counter this. Theft leaves you defenseless, so the first step is to reassure yourself of your own strength. There are only two kinds of people who can trust. One is those who have never had their trust betrayed. The others are the strong ones, the battle scared who learn to trust again who learn to recoup or reclaim everything intangible that was taken. You are not powerless. Realise this and don't rebuild a karma of hate, in place of the trust and self value and other things you have lost, because such a thing will damage you more, It will give more power to thief for they will have taken not only our money, or idea or property's but something of yourself.

The karma and psychology to be worked on is sometimes about helpless or powerless, rather than money, a lack of respect in life, it may be linked with non financial situations where you have been made to feel the same. If the thief is known to you, it may reflect situations about self worth, betrayal and about being used, or exploited, or abused, the value others place on you. These may go deep into other areas of your past or life and need to be worked on as well as the actual theft. The healing process involves regaining of power and self value, and the respect of others. The healing and cleansing of the spirit. The very process of work on self value, will raise your confidence, your status and finally your bank balance, though it can be a long task

Success is the Best Revenge

Lastly anger and a craving for revenge can be a legacy of theft but it is destructive too, and can perpetuate bad karma though it's a natural enough reaction. I don't know who first said this, but it's a famous saying I find it very therapeutic, like a healing mantra to deal with this kind of anger if you say it proudly and from the heart, it works. I think you will find it healing and uplifting too; "success is the best revenge". I know you will succeed. This is my wish for you. Do well and be happier with you life in every possible way, than they are with theirs, not just financially but totally, to seen by your enemies to be doing well. Anger and revenge are healthy fighting emotions, survival emotions. It is depression you have to watch for, depression is a defeat emotion. If depression sets in after a theft, you're not surviving very well.

Astrologically Neptune and Mercury rule thieves, confidence tricksters, deception makers of all kinds. To avoid theft, look out for difficult transit aspects, squares, quincunx, oppositions, to the ruler of your houses of money, to the second house cusp, to aspects made from second house transits to your Sun, ruling planet, or second and eighth house ruler. Look out for similar difficult synastry aspects. If for example someone's Neptune falls in your second house or conjuncts your Jupiter, this person will either be deceptive about money matters or may steal from you, or at best may just be an idle or foolish sort who is a drain on your income in one way another, this is a synastry aspect that becomes more important in business partnerships.

If you have Neptune or Mercury aspecting your tenth cusp, or in your tenth house. Beware of your business partners. Business partners, agents and associates of your work do not always swindle in a straight forward way, as I have learned to my cost. Neptune is never straight forward. They thieve by exploitation, by building a business on your back, by taking the lion's share of profits, or getting you to sign away all your rights. Thieve by dubious agreements, by unkept promises, trickery, treachery, and occasionaly by neglect. These are all very Neptunian things. There is many a pop star whose agent takes millions while he struggles to pay the rent. I recall reading about one very famous band, whose musical royalty's amounted to a penny, the smallest coin in England, a penny for each record sold! Though I can actually top that from my own early experiences!

I was commissioned to write a book, received a one off payment that amounted to a couple of weeks income, no royalties, no further payments. I didn't think much about it at the time. My clients told me it went into a second edition, and it still continues to be re printed and rehashed with different name over the years for which I receive zilch; absolutely nothing at all. An amusing side light that actually would probably shock the publisher was the book took me approximately only a couple of months to write, while still keeping up with my clients demands. I had to cut so much out of the book to make it short enough for what the agent who commissioned me wanted it to be, that there was another volume left over in scraps alone. I could have written them ten more! Exploitation is robbery. When we are robbed by agents, publishers, business partners, companies, big business, we can blame our own folly or naivety in part. It's hard being a goldfish in a shark pool. There are karmic and worldly lessons to learn on both sides. If you have a strong Saturn you'll learn through experience, if you have a strong Neptune you will be fooled every time. A good Uranus and you might just turn the tables.

An artist is uniquely talented in his art, and will always be unique, will always have a trade, one that no one else can reproduce, will be uplifting to others and inspiring. An artist has many works of art within his soul. Unscrupulous companies, and agents, dishonest partners and opportunistic exploiters build bad karma and fail to see how they themselves lose out in the end. It goes full circle, like the stars. Their gain, is a tiny drop in the ocean, but the loss to them is what they *could* have gained. People who are exploited don't always have the means to fight back, or the voice to make themselves heard. But karma always completes itself.

Aspects of Dishonesty

We all subconsciously engineer our own destiny. When you aim at wealth, aim at true wealth. Wealth of money, wealth of the soul. There is also the other side of the coin, when the bad prosper it's because the good nothing.

Here's what to look out for

When comparing your chart with a partner's, in Synastry, a Square, Quincunx or hard aspects between your Jupiter and the other person's Neptune, in an area of your chart to do with money, often means dishonesty. Similar aspects between Pluto and Jupiter can also result in your being scammed or conned or suffering great losses. Watch out under these transits aspects too, be very carefull in all your financial affairs when you have transit Jupiter in a negative aspect to your Pluto, or Neptune.

Gold-diggers

If the ruler of the seventh house, the house of partnerships in your chart falls in your second house you may be conned out of money by your partner, but not necessarily, much will depend on the synastry between your chart and the other's. The aspect just shows the potential so you need to take extra financial care in partnerships. It's not always a bad aspect or indeed a theft aspect, If it's Mars or Venus, you may pay for sex, whether you intended to pay or not! Most of us at some time in life are familiar with "The expensive date", the gold digging girl or boy, who is great fun, a social aesthete, but terribly costly, always wanting this and that, and always ready to move on to someone richer once you have been fleeced. Such arrangements can be more subtle and many people have a love affair but end up unwillingly financing a long term lover,. The same aspect more positively can mean, you "buy" yourself a husband, mistress or wife. Whether the subsequent marriage is happy, and is for more than the money on the spouses part, depends on the synastry.

Con-men

Chiron in Quincunx to Jupiter. Chiron in hard aspect to Jupiter in your natal chart, warns you could be conned out of a vast amount of money at various times in life (those times show by malefic transits, or can be worked out by progression and other methods of predicting the future and so can warn you in advance).

Pluto in the house of money, or eighth house, means extremes of fate, great loss or great gain, the feast or the famine, so he should be watched carefully.

Doing a Runner

Neptune in the fourth house is another one to watch. When badly aspected by Chiron, it can mean loss of property, deception in the home. One client born with Neptune in the fourth, her boyfriend, unknown to her, stopped paying the rent on their flat, hid the final demand notices and eviction orders and court orders. The day before the bailiff knocked on the door was the day he did a runner. Her Natal Neptune was that year very badly aspected by a malefic transit that included Chiron aspects. When there are aspects from Chiron or Neptune to the fourth house by transit, property deals often go terribly wrong, the wool is pulled over your eyes. You make decisions you regret, you are surrounded by untrustworthy people, those you live with cannot be trusted, but you don't see through their lies until it's too late. Chiron often means loss of a property unfairly. While Neptune means you cannot put your trust in situation to do with the home. Situations to do with Neptune happen slowly over a long period, the loss and deception is veiled and only found in the culmination of events. Pluto the slower moving planet by contrast moves fast with loss, is the axe man, his losses are quick sudden, in one fell swoop.

Watch Neptune

Where ever transit Neptune is in your chart that is where you are most vulnerable to deception and loss. Where Neptune aspects is also another loss. For example if Radix Neptune aspects your tenth house cusp, there is exploitation, or deception in the work place, this exploitation will come to light when the aspect is triggered by a transit. Neptune transits last a long time, but they will only bring an event of loss when Neptune makes an aspect to a malefic during that transit, thus you can time dangerous events and losses and try to avoid them. If he is transition the second of eighth house the losses, risks and deceptions will surely be financial.

When he transits the fourth house, the losses and deceptions will be around the home, and may or may not be financial, but it is wise to take care in any property deals, rents, mortgages, home repairs, insurances, and pensions this is where you may be ripped off. The fourth house has an influence over the " end of life" as well as home and property, and so pension funds, your will, and aspects of inheritance come under this house too. Members of your household may also pull the wool over your eyes, so may parents. In the third and ninth house, its siblings, and legal matters, cars and vehicles you have to watch and mistrust and all things to do with them, in the tenth, employment matters.

Redundancy's, theft at work, co workers, legality's to do with employers may be deceptive, again it may not be financial for Neptune rules many things, but being the house of employment it could have financial repercussions.

The twelfth house has to do with pensions. Neptune in the twelfth aspecting the tenth or sixth cusp, can predict the loss of a works or state pension.

Retrograde Jupiter

Especially in a money house or in a hard aspect to Pluto. This planet when retrograde can take money from you rather than give it. So it warns you to be cautious against losses. Pluto is also traumatic ending and new beginnings,, so it warns you that at some point in life plans to make a brave new beginning in life, such as emigration, new business, may not work out due to a financial reversal or dishonesty, excess money being taken from you, to make this new beginning. A bottomless pit. It doesn't mean you cannot succeed and become wealthy in life but it does warn you to be cautious when this hard aspect is activated by a difficult transit. Timing and misting of such a venture can be everything.

Stock Market Trading

This is the chart of a client who makes his living from stock market trading, on the internet. This is the kind of high risk business that most astrologers would advise against. But his chart is a good one and I think it's the right business for him. He is successful at it, He also has a background in banking.

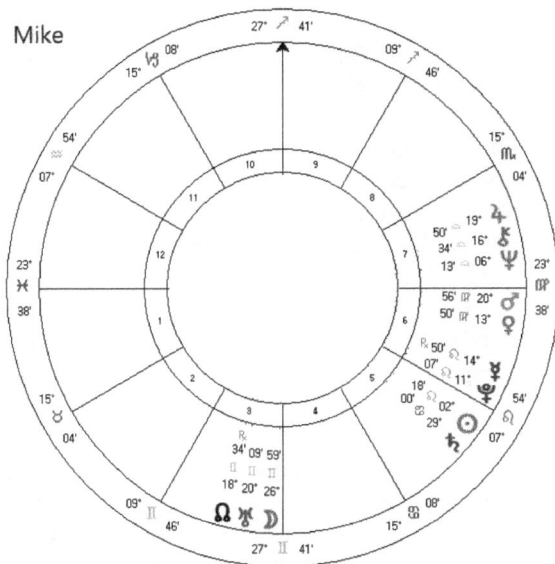

Mike

Mike has Scorpio on the 8th house cusp. Scorpio is a sign that is at home with the occult, the hidden, the psychic, the underworld. This means he is intuitively aware and perceptive of the economic trends, the money markets and what's going on behind the scenes of the world financially. This is a good sign for anyone who works with money at all to have. He is good at predicting financial trends, especially hidden ones that run like dark eels in water or like currents or below the surface of the world of money. This is his real talent. He also has the Sun in the fifth house. In the financial chart the fifth house, is gambling, risk, speculation. The Sun is never bad. A Sun can be afflicted and it's goodness hampered by other planets, but it is never itself bad. A person with the Sun in the first house; house of self, is essentially a good person, no matter what happens in their life to make them sad, mad or deviant. A person with the Sun in the fifth house is a good gambler. Traditionally it means he will gain through gambling and risk taking.

The Scorpion is a nice sign to have in the eighth house for dealings with stocks and bonds. Pluto, Scorpios ruler is also the planet of becoming an authority in ones work. So he will become rather expert at his knowledge of stocks

The Fifth House is strong in his chart. This house is about games of chance, risk. This can also include artistic pursuits, hobbies, games gambling and sports. It is about winning, and the competitive instincts. This can be on a physical level or a mental level. With Pisces, a water sign rising, it is more likely to manifest, as it has in mental competitiveness. In his life the stocks and shares fit with that trait. Gambling successfully goes right through his chart in many ways like a vein of colour through a marble slab. It is what he was born to do. But if he wants to be totally happy there may be a need to bring out his creative or artistic or "people" side, to fill the other side of this aspect. Some people say a strong fifth house confers an element of luck both to life and working situations. This chart is a successful one.

These same financial aspects when applied to a chart of a big business rather than to the chart of a man, especially the Pluto ones, are successful for businesses such as a firm of insurance brokers. It's much better influence for an insurance company to have Scorpio on its eighth house, than for say a bank to have it there. Pluto is a baleful planet, he has a forensic darkness about him, in ordinary astrology he rules trauma, fear, death, disaster. Sudden ending and bleak new beginnings. These are all Pluto things and insurances make their living from implanting in the collective mind the murky and impalpable fear of what might happen, what we must guard against and how it can be turned into money when it does. The first person to invent insurance must surely have been one of the all time financial greats! I don't know who it was, though I'm sure someone will e-mail or write and tell me!. He or she was able to sell a commodity without substance, he or she sold fear and uncertainty along with its antidote, turned thin air into money and into the forerunner of a dark restrictive plague on the planet. For many things we once enjoyed, or let our children enjoy from carnival floats to rambling markets, to playing in the snow, are now sadly diminished because of a gullible and greedy society that sues everything inside out and perpetuates the insurance rip off. How fitting for a financial institution whose profit revolves round insurance sales or claims in any form is an eighth house Scorpio. While a bank, or investment institutions prospers more with an eighth house Sagittarius.

To return to Mike's chart. If Mike wanted another financial side line to augment his earnings, becoming a mortgage broker, dealing with house or building insurance company's, rents or leases, would pay off for him. Better than for example trying to sell pension schemes (which come under Capricorn, i. e. old age, even if some are insurance based). If a person works with the signs and planets in their chart they maximize their success in both the small and big things. With his Moon at the nadir it is suggested that he is going to eventually have two lines of work not one. The Moon in the fourth house is also property, housing, and homes. Though may just be something he takes up temporarily or occasionally. The Moon has little permanency in a financial chart, it is like a flickering candle, that can change randomly, it comes into force when it's well aspected by transits and then it draws gains, new ventures, success for a time, or it fills a gap, until the fluctuation alters and then it wavers like a guttering light bringing losses or dwindlings when badly aspected. A Moon can be a tide of opportunity, or a tide of loss. So his Moon is like a second string to his income, something held in reserve, but not permanent that he will call upon from time to time to advance himself or fill a gap in his finances when needed.

So while the stock market is Mike's main line of work, and success, there is going to be a second income or second string to his bow, possibly to do with property, or property investing. This will bring out a different side of his character, but may not necessarily be a big money earner. The satisfaction in it could come from using a different talent or different part of the mind, The Sun is the self, the Moon being the consort of the Sun, is the other side of our self

In his chart the Sun in the fifth house, house of speculation is close enough to aspect the sixth house cusp, house of working life. This means that he is better equipped than most to make his income and lifework from gambling. The Sun is strong being his ruling planet, it makes him practical and down to earth in his stock dealings. If he'd had say Neptune here instead and as his ruler, then it would be dreams delusion, addiction and, gullibility and too much gambling. The tendency to loss too much. His chart, with Virgo and its ruler Mercury occupying the other part of the sixth house, shows he will pursue his Career goals in a practical and methodical " Virgoan" manner, carefull self controlled, detail orientated and accurately. Those are Virgo traits. He may be critical in the face of opposition to his goals and methods and his Leo Sun may make him too proud to admit failures at times. But his exacting and precise accurate way of working will bring those ambitions to successes

His MC. or tenth house ruler forms a square, to his fifth. Jupiter is in Libra in his seventh, showing a happy marriage that can withstand fluctuations of income. The square, or Mike's work will create tensions, in the marriage, but this square is not negative. It is off set by other aspects. Mike's success will be such that his business will eventualy bring them a better home or better environment (Jupiter - Uranus, also Moon and Venus aspects in the chart, all linked to home, environment and ending of difficulty's, Uranus ruler of twelfth house of difficulty's)

For those interested in stocks, or for investing in other peoples business. Aspects between the planets show the trends of the market. Good aspects, show good trends, bad ones difficulties. Aspects may be slow moving planets show long term trends. Quick moving ones fluctuation and short term.

Stocks and type of business to invest in

Aries

Iron, steel, diamonds, cars, motors and engineering. Armaments, weapons, beer and spirit. Wool, and woolen products. Products of war. Roofing products. Charities or Organizations to do with wars. Sports companies, sports clothing and equipment.

Taurus

Currency exchange, financial trusts, banks, leather, beef, butter, milk, cheese. Banks and money, building societies, credit unions.

Gemini

Newspapers, publishing, telecommunications, print. Post offices. Mail and package delivery services. Library's, archives of all kinds. Books, Bookbinding, Languages and literacy. Recording. Fashion shops and chain stores. Taxi's and short distance transport.

Cancer

Nationalized industries. Catering. Food industry. Dairies. Domestic appliances. Yogurt, Milk, Oysters, Baby foods and equipment. Women's interests. Property. Children's homes. Grocery shops and supermarkets. Breweries. Real estate.

Leo

Gold, theatrical and sporting interests, gilt edged stocks, DVDs, recording and television equipment. Gaming gambling, betting and lotterys. Theatre, acting and its requirements. Companies with Royal patronage.

Virgo.

Medicines and medical. Linen, cloth, dyes. Wheat, Corn. Agricultural crops. The service industry's, Organizations and Charity's for pets and small animals. Pet foods, Cleaning and hygiene industry and products.

Libra.

Copper, accessories, luxury and decorative goods. Jewelry, precious and semi precious stones. Luxury fabrics. Decorative glass. Beauty products.

Scorpio.

Insurances, atomic industry, vacuum cleaners, gas, oil, coal, minerals. Drains, drainage.

Submarines. Nuclear industry. Poisonous and toxic substance. Sewage systems. Black onyx, Jett, funeral industry. Underwear, sex industry.

Sagittarius.

Foot ball, Book makers and betting, Team sports. Race horses. Large Company's and chains that have their origins in a different country. Travel industry.

Capricorn.

Timber, Recycling. Tool makers. Old people's homes. History. Old Documents. Charity's for the poor or needy Sheds. Wooden buildings, including flat pack houses, chalet's beach huts, and American " Trailer homes "

Aquarius.

Arts, New inventions. Technology and computer interests.

Wind mills and wind power. Turbines, Fans, Eco systems, and Green economy. Water purification systems.

Pisces.

Refrigeration, preservatives, anesthetic drugs, shoes, stockings.

brewers, intoxicating liquors, fish and Fishery's, hospitals, institutions, prisons, all nursing home requirements, such as bandages, beds. Hospitals and institutions, Naval and shipping concerns.

Sun.

Government stocks, gold, brass, old currency's like sovereigns. Lighting companies.

Moon.

Silver, platinum. Water. Soft drinks, land and property.

Mercury.

Newspapers, Magazines, municipal stock, plastics, printers. / postage stamps. Sound equipment. Children's charity's and children's organizations. Communications. Red lead, Mercury. Amalgams and alloys.

Venus

Copper, art, sugar. Amusements, jewelers. Prostitution. The sex industry. Luxury cloths. Cosmetics. Hair products.

Mars

Iron and steel. Cars, motors, engineering, weapons, Football, baseball, rugby. Furnaces. Fire service. Knives blades and swords. Ovens. Incinerators. Surgical equipment. Sharp instruments. Butchers.

Jupiter

Overseas shares, paper and publishing. Horse racing. Hotels. Trees. New Timber. Legal and civil law. Church.

Saturn

Coal, bricks, cement, building materials, lead. Watches and clocks. Tin, Iron. Lead, Pottery. Clay or earth. Burial grounds. Undertakers' requirements. Aged people's homes, alms houses, and charities or organizations to do with the old and aged. Cloths that are work a day.

Chiron.

Medicines, sports, body fluids. Abortion. Charity's for people who are lacking something. The homeless, amputees. Also charity's for infantile death, cot death, miscarriages

Uranus,

Electrical, scientific, computer technologies, Aircraft. Trains, Railways. Robotics, internet. Windmills. Electronics. Public utilities. New inventions. Asylums for the criminally insane. Polonium. Radium. Charity's for natural disasters, like earthquake. Warning systems for flood, earth quake, and natural disasters. New inventions. Organizations to do with reform.

Neptune

Liquids and distillers. Chemicals, Oil wells, also rape oil and vegetable oils, liquid gas, petrol, drugs and pharmaceuticals, tobacco, cotton, tea, coffee, rice, cotton, Flax and linen, ships, glass, Water. Coco. Mental hospitals. Toxic liquids. Fishers and Fish farms. Shipping, and water transport.

Pluto

Fossils, oil, nuclear technology, power or energy utility's. X rays, microwaves, magnetic imaging. Scanning equipment, generators, and septic tanks. Mining, coal and oil. Construction and demolition shares, armaments bombs, nuclear power. Space travel. Recycling, submarines.

Nodes

Film, television, glamour industry's. Camera companies. Holograms.

In stocks, world markets and high finance Transit Saturn in an earth sign, is a loss of money, especially in worldly or earthy things, and loss of livestock. In a water sign, watery things go down, ships, oil from below the sea. In air signs, things depend on the air waves, radio, internet, planes, air raft sometimes go down, and in fire it's as one would expect, all the combustibles, the fuel, the intelectual goods. With Jupiter transits these go up.

Combinations of planets, or planets in signs can also show particular things due to their rulerships and signatures, for example, Venus and Neptune together, rules silks, perfumes. Venus being luxurious goods and Neptune smoothness. Venus in Taurus rules fur. Uranus and Saturn, rules antique. Saturn and the Moon, pewter, for Saturn is lead and the Moon silver and so on. There are many such combinations, some are well known, some you can only learn by experience, by keeping your own research notes, by following the stock market, and business training news and if you do that time will teach you to pinpoint more astrological significators. The more you refine your own system of trading, the more accurate and yielding your investments will become

Look to the rulers of the first and second house, and the transiting Moon, if the transit Moon is separating from a good aspect from the ruler of the eighth house and applying to the ruler of the second, it is a good time to buy stocks and shares. If the transiting ruler of the eighth house is in good aspect to the ruler of the second and the transiting ruler of the second in good aspect to radix Jupiter, Moon, or Venus, it is favourable to buy or sell stocks and shares. If the ruler of the second afflicts the ruler of the eighth by a bad transit aspect you can buy or sell. It is not advisable to buy, when there is a transiting malefic in the first, second, seventh, or eighth house, Unless that malefic is the ruler of the first house, or second house. If the ruler of the seventh is transiting in bad aspect to the ruler of first or second, do not buy.

If the ruler of the seventh house falls in the second by transit, you may lose or the shares devalue.

When to buy.

When the ruler of the second is in good aspect to the ruler of the eighth house., or when the transit Moon aspect both rulers favorably. When the ruler of the second house conjuncts the eighth house cusp. It is also a good time to buy when the transit Moon is separating from the ruler of the eighth house, and moving away from a bad aspect, into a good aspect with the ruler of the second house.

When to sell.

When a beneficial planet is transiting the second house and the ruler of the first house is in the seventh. The Moon going from a good aspect to the ruler of the second, into a bad aspect to the ruler of the seventh or eighth. When the ruler of the first goes into the seventh house.

The Money Chart

The work of analyzing an astrology chart, is only ever partly visible to the client. It is not simply the aspects that appear in the chart that I base my conclusions on, but also the ones that don't. Nothing is ever written about these, they take up no space in the report given to the client but they still take time to assess, If you are reading this book and reading your own chart you must be just as scrupulous because there are aspects which if they did arise they would make a big difference to the outcome of your question.

I always look at the psychological aspects. Because in a chart like the sample one, where the client had wanted to know if he would be successful enough in stock market trading to earn his living from it. I have to look to see if there is an addictive or obsessive aspect, something dormant in his character that could rise up later on and lead the client to ruin, but that isn't the case here. If another person were going into say work for a political " Cause" Id look at her chart for tendency for fanaticism, a dangerous proclivity that could turn a good thing bad and lead tragedy. These things have to be assessed, because we want the client's success to be permanent not transitory.

Gambling in any form can be an insidious disease that poisons the future and leads to ruin. It is true that gambling can make you rich, but your addiction to it never will. Breaking that addiction is one step closer to wealth. There are some charts that show chronic debt that comes from a paralyzing weakness of the soul, it may be an addiction, it may be a moldering fear. The client may not have asked about it but these aspects have to be looked for before any total judgment about a future can be made. This is all part of the silent or invisible work that the astrologer does which client has little conception of. If you're reading your own chart try to be just as thorough. How will wealth or poverty or risk taking affect your partner, your home, your happiness, your family, your future plans, your health and wellbeing. Look at all the aspects, the whole chart, you want to know the total picture.

To maximize your success by astrology can make you a billionaire, or it may merely keep you from sinking down for a time, for much also hangs on your own ability's and force of character to keep afloat, or to rise to greatness. We can never know untill afterwards how much an astrological financial chart reading helps a person, but it can never harm.

In analysing the financial chart, I look at are ways to maximize your success, by using the planets and aspects positively, and trying to re balance any that seem to be acting negatively, Planets that seem to compel your subconscious towards poverty, or spoil or destroying the opportunity's wealth in your life, this is how the book came to be written, I cannot help each one of you individually there are too many countless millions, but my book can reach more of you. Why you? Why do I want to make you rich, because money is power, and if you are reading this book you are in some way spiritual and a richer you can make the world a better place for all of us. Also I want to give you some of my wealth and the wealth I have is my knowledge.

In true astrological tradition a money reading can give lucky colours, numbers, gems, and dates and days when to begin or end transaction. It can pin point lucky times, when it's wise to gamble, or trade on the stock market, when it's wise to invest or to sell. In short astrology may not have all the answers but it can help pinpoint when there is a greater chance of that individual winning.

Interpreting the business chart

Money and business should be happily married. I shall write a further book about business astrology and maximizing your success in business, for those who, want to work for themselves, or want to become company's or small business. It is a complex subject, and so in this money book I have included only a glimmering, but enough to get you started on what can be an engrossing study. Financial success in business can be developed and maximized in a similar way, to personal monetary gain, and follows similar rules and observations. However we have to read the same chart differently. In this book I will only give a sketchy outline for those advanced enough in astrology to begin the process of a business chart.

What the houses means in a business chart

First House
This is the image of the business, the name of the business, its colors and its beginnings. For example; Saturn in Scorpio, an occult or hidden business began in poverty, what the business has to cope with in its personal life.

Second House,

The business aesthetes, money and profits, if prosperity will come and when and where from, accumulation of wealth, the value of the product or job or work well done.

Third House.

Advertising and communications, the accounts, your ability to learn new things that will be useful in your business, your accountant, your rivals and competitors.

Fourth House,

the building or premises from which the business, is conducted. Properties owned by the business. Its website. The base of the business, its country, town, its influence on that town if any, its location, any real estate.

Fifth House.

business risks, and speculations of the business, also what will develop or emerge or evolve out of the business in the future, this being the traditional house of the child, it is how the business will grow. Any family, children, or steps that will follow you into the business.

Sixth House,

the day to day work. The health of the business and the way the clients' health will effect or influence it. How you deal with your customers or clients and co workers, your work habits.

Seventh House.

Business partners, agents and equal status or symbiotic helpers.

Eighth House.

Taxation and expenses, what is borrowed, what the business owes, also the history of the business, or history of the kind of work, house of debts and shared resources, how you value your stock, your goods, your service, if you over or undervalue, the expenses of the business and it's upkeep, main expenses, and it's waste.

Ninth House.

exports, the business banking its finances and expansions, its foreign trade, or its long distance trade, advertising and distribution, foreign markets for your work.

Tenth House.

The character of the business; the job of work, the task, the business and it's nature, what it is achieving, also the client as it's boss, The reputation you will achieve and you public success, any publicity or fame for your work or business will show here.

Eleventh House

The aspirations of the business, what you eventually hope will happen. This house represents the customers or the contented clients of the business. Groups, casual association of benefit to the business. Symbiotic businesses.

Twelfth House

Any mail order interests of the business. The difficulties of the business, and also its secrets, retirement plans, the post or mail. Difficult customers Research and development of the business.

There are three good ways to draw up a Business chart but this list of house meanings is used, whichever method of erecting the Chart is selected.

Erecting The Business Chart.

Determining the birth time of a business in order to construct its chart is debatable. It is rather like

98

determining the birth time of a nation, to read the future England, or America. If the right time is not chosen then the chart will not work. And nay interpretation will be a misinterpretation however skillfully done. If you're a profession astrologer the client will tell you the time he or she considers or believes to be its birth time, and that is an excellent time to use, for however arbitrary the client ahs chosen the moment, the client has a greater intuitive link with his own business than you do. He will inwardly know the right time, just as a mother intrusively recognizes when her own baby is ill, even if the doctor has said it isn't sick. Only if he faulters or thinks too much about it or is too wavering in certainty will you have the misfortune to be called to decide the right time.

If your deciding the time, you have many choices.. Is it the day papers are signed and a limited company formed ? Is it the day the door of the shop opens and trading begins? The moment the first customer pays, the moment two friends in a public house discus the idea of setting up their own business? The moment the name is chosen, is that when the business comes into being? There are many dates and times to choose from, so many it's a wonder a business chart can be done with nay accuracy at all. There is a date when the business premises are rented or web site launched and so on. There is no hard and fast rule, much as astrologers would like one. Basically if the chart works, that is if it appears to describe the nature of the business and the circumstance, yourself as the proprietor, any other people and places involved, if it shows clearly the premises you work from and all the known circumstances of that business at present, use it. Because it will portray the future just as accurately as it describes the circumstances..

If it doesn't seem to fit. Take one of the other significant dates as the nativity of the business. It may later be revealed to your satisfaction why the other date is the significant one..

Not all traders can recall when their business began, this is not a problem. Other methods with sole traders, are to take one of the approximate dates, for example "the business began in November, last year" but use the sign and degree of the clients midhaven, as the degree on the ascendant for the " last November" chart, Since the midhaven is the persons house of businessman the ascendant is the beginning of things, and he began the business. So this way you have your year and time of birth. You then have to decide which particular day of "last November" is the appropriate day. So you look at the clients chart and at the *transit* aspects for that November. You look for anything significant that might spell out a new enterprise. A person doesn't begin a business every day. Where there any major aspects? Aspects that doesn't happen often? Or did the ruler of his the tenth or sixth house conjunct his Sun, linking himself with work issues? Did a planet conjunct he cusp of the money house? If the month is correct there will be some outstanding aspect, Use the day of the aspect for the day of the chart. The result will be a chart that is a constructed or manufactured chart, it may not be the actual beginning of the business, but it will work because it represents the business more closely than anything.

If the person is the sole trader, or is himself the business, a lot can be told by using the above list of houses as a template over the natal chart, and reading the persons chart in relation to his business this way. The man and the microcosm. The business as a reflection of the self. Someone with Saturn it the first house will have a serious business image, or a poor image or a difficult impoverished start to the business, because Saturn rules both poverty and seriousness and the first house in the business chart is image, it's beginnings. While someone with Venus there may have a more light-hearted one, may employ beuatifull art work to get his image going, the help of creative friends and so on.

These are just clues, crumbs for the advanced astrologer, in another book I will elaborate on astrology and the running of your own business. For the moment and purpose of this book financial astrology and business astrology are not at all inseparable they simple over lap in certain places, just as poverty and wealth can overlap in peoples lives and have a place in the money book. Not everyone views running their own business as the way to get wealthy and indeed the attempt can make some people poorer. There are ways to avoid that, but this book has to concentrate its efforts on personal wealth.

Increase your Wealth using Moon Cycles

Over a period of time the Moon has an influence on the growth and diminishment of all things, including money. You don't need a deep knowledge of astrology to begin to put few simple astrological rules into practice in your life. These rules will help your money improve and increase.

New Moon.

The new Moon initiates a cycle of endings and beginnings, a time of change. Financial matters and pending business matters are better finished before the new Moon. The new Moon is the time to being new financial venture.

It is good for ending financial affairs and matters that you want to remain secret. For hiding money. For stowing it away. Dissolving financial ties. For making intuitive guesses and prediction about money matters. Good time for starting new financial and business ventures.

Waxing Moon.

The waxing Moon promotes growth of financial matters. This is a good period to begin new ventures of money projects that involve increase or a wish for gain. As the Moon grows so will your endevours Prosperity rituals blessing for a business or venture.

Full Moon

The full Moon brings to fruition the things that were initiated around the time of the new Moon or before. The glow of the full Moon sheds its light on situations that you could not see clearly before. So it is a good time for examining your financial matters and plans, reading contracts, or understanding difficult matters. Bringing monetary things to their maturity or their conclusion.

Waning Moon.

The waning Moon assists decrease. This two week period is an advantageous time to do things that involve the reduction of things. This is the time to pay bills,, end a financial contract. To pay debts. As the Moon light decreases so will whatever you do at this time. During this time you can refine projects and systems and follow up projects you initiated during the waxing Moon. Make repairs, so that if you owe someone compensation, now is the time.

These cycles will always be more powerfull when the Moon falls in your second house, or eighth house sign. When in the tenth for business matter, and the fourth for home matters. So a full Moon in your tenth house for example would be good for concluding a business deal, winding up the debts of a business Or closing it down. While a full Moon in the fourth would have its strongest influence over your domestic finances. An eclipse of the Moon in any house of sign is not good, and action and decisions are best avoided in that month. In stocks and share dealing an eclipse can mean a sudden fall. But this brings us into very advanced astrology which is outside the realm of this book.

Everyone without astrological knowledge can work financially and successfully with the changing Moon. You only need a diary that has the Moons phases a newspaper that gives them to be able to know what stage the Moon is at. You can also look at the Moon in the sky at night, you will soon become adept at knowing the difference between a full Moon, that is perfectly round and an almost full Moon that isn't quite perfectly round!

If you have some additional knowledge of astrology you can also work with its signs and houses in your chart. If you do so, you will soon see good results in your material affairs, they will improve gradually, and debts will diminish. New money will arrive. When a thing is done at the right time, it will have the right result.

Bitter fruit

In your life you have seen less deserving people prosper. You have watched doors open for them, and usher in a better life, while you have stood like a beggar on the threshold. You have seen them being given the chances that you never were given yourself but deserved so much more than them. You may have worked hard while they idled, you may have worn rags while they wore precious cloths and gold. You may know you are a better person spiritually a good person, while they are not. But to be bitter envious or angry is not the way forward. It will hold you back like a shackle. For who is to say it's nit the envy in your soul that is detracting form wealth, that this is not some kind of karmic restraint that will be with you until you learn better. Do not begrudge anyone else their success or their money, or the easy way they are able live. To pour hatred into your poverty, is to make yourself spiritually poorer as well as financially poorer.

This is not the path to wealth; Lack of money will diminish the quality of you material life but don't allow it to damage or diminish your spiritual life, or to diminish yourself as a person. To do so creates negative karma in the world, it let's darkness triumph and helps greed, envy, dishonesty and other destructive things take over; the path to personal wealth is a path to power, such things that darken your spirit will act like a stumbling block to becoming rich. So wealth may be withheld untill you overcome such feelings. If you become rich and are full of hate you will misuse the power of wealth, and perpetuate the destructive mean side of wealth as so many people do in the world. You are better than this. That may be what the karma of poverty is about for you, wealth may be the reward for overcoming envy, avarice, greed. We cannot escape karma but we can work with it. Only your individual chart will show what your karma of comprises of.

Your soul is aware of the injustices you see. So let it rest at that. These other destructive emotions do not belong with happiness, power or wealth and anything that does not belong to wealth is an obstacle to the obtaining of wealth.

Astrologically; Mars aspect to the Sun, cause envy. Professional or career envy is often signified by Mars aspect in or to the tenth house. Mars in the earth sign are more prone to envy, while an obsessive pernicious envy will include Pluto and possibly Neptune in the equation somewhere.

Lucky Jupiter

Jupiter is the planet of luck. He is seldom bad, but if Jupiter rules your house of money, his influence must be considered. Look to where he is placed in your chart.

Ninth house.

Finances will be fortune in the second half of life. You may gain money from Spiritual or religious occupations' from being a teacher, mentor, guru. Lawyer or educator. You will benefit from foreign countries and people at a distance, if this planet is well aspected or strong. But if unfavorably aspected or weak, a lack of higher education hinders earning ability. You may not afford a teacher without going into debts, and any law suits are liable to be unfavorable in outcome to you. There is loss by religions or faith. The advice with an unfavorable Jupiter so you can correct the patters of fate, would be try not to break the law, try not to go to legal disputes if you can settle the situation in some other way. Don't drop out of education, see it through and get the qualifications you need.

Fifth House.

The potential for great gain or loss through gambling and speculation. When Jupiter is badly aspected, he is unlucky in this house, and his normally good potential won't work for you. It is an advice not to take risks.

Jupiter and religion

Every planet governs more than one thing in life. Jupiter as a planet rules faith. It can be the faith in a religion, or belief in a political cause. He rules outer wealth but also the essence of inner guidance,. He rules teachers, but of the kindly sort, as opposed to Saturn who is the strict stern teacher, he rules the law, the government, parental figures, all those who one way and another guide us and lead us and keep us in order. But has not Pluto the dictator. Or Neptune the dreamer. There is the conception that materialism and spirituality are opposite things. That one cannot be both spiritual and materialistic. This is not totally true. I always say to people, if you have two legs, you walk. You would not think of hopping everywhere unless you were forced to do so by misfortune. Recognise that the material and financial side of life are equal. That one is as important as the other. The material side is as important as the spiritual side.

Both things make the world. The glamour side of the city and its wealth and decadence, and the natural simplicity and peace of its gardens and trees. They are often opposite but the same. The spiritual and natural. The material and the mental. To live for one and not the other is like hopping on one leg when you could be walking on two. There is the spiritual and there is the material, never think of abandoning one for the other, you must use both in balance. If Jupiter, the planet of both wealth and the planet of spiritual things was to guide you, if he was a god this would be his message. Because this is his meaning.

Jupiter's violinist

When should you beware of beautifull benign Jupiter? Jupiter is law, authority, and convention, so if your fiddling, embezzling, falsifying, thieving or being criminal in your finances, keep a wary watchfull eye on Jupiter transits. Jupiter is the upholder of Justice. If it is justice that you should thieve, then Jupiter may let you get you get away with it, but the moment you take to much, or from the wrong source, the planet will become negative and your come upance will arrive. Jupiter is the jovial Father Christmas, with his stout red coat and beard as white as snow and benign smile. Father Christmas gives gingerbread and presents to all the good children, but what some people don't know is that Mother Christmas follows is his wake on her own sinister dark sledge with her icicle fingers and she doesn't give gingerbread, she punishes the bad children!

Jupiter is always a gamble. A risk. He is not judgmental he is the bringer of joy, But he can pass us by empty handed, or he can bring something nasty following in his steps if we haven't been good. Jupiter connected with Uranus is especially so. Uranus is a planet that can turn the tables on you. She can reverse things, so can Mercury. And Neptune. Mercury is the trickster, Neptune the thief but if your fiddling or thieving or embezzling then the trickster is usualy yourself, so it's more when Jupiter or Uranus are stacked against Mercury, or your Sun, or your money houses that you have to watch out! If Neptune or Saturn transits the twelfth house at the same time, and your crime is bad enough then prison can loom.

Jupiter's great enemy

Experience of many charts has led me to believe that Saturn and Jupiter have a natural antipathy. So Jupiter will not bring much luck to the house Saturn rules in your chart, even when he is good aspect or transiting., anything he brings will be weakened or blocked somewhat. The same to the house Saturn sits in. If you have Saturn or Capricorn in your third house, little luck will come from your education, even if it was a good one, nothing much will proceed from it. The old school tie will not advance you very far. The knowledge gained there may not be the knowledge that will use for your success in life. If Saturn or Capricorn is in your fifth house then there is little happiness or fugal gain through children, there may be no children or only loss. There is a paucity of gain by gambling. Jupiter does not do his best work either by transit or by aspect when Saturn or Saturn's sign is there

If you have Saturn conjunct the Sun, or were born under Capricorn, Jupiter is a less lucky planet for you and wont necessarily bring as much or exactly what he seems to promise in your chart or by transit, but conversely Saturn, who is the noted bad boy of astrology and who doesn't generally bestow much luck by transit or aspect, will bring good fortune to your door.

Partnership or working for yourself

For some people the transformative root to money and success is through beginning their own business. Your own business can rid you of limitations and restrictions and bring opportunity that conventional employment sometimes cannot. If your attitude to your work is right your abilities will reach a maximum of effectiveness and good results will inevitably follow. If you do that which is in your soul to do, success will follow. To work at something not suited, or among unsuitable people and conditions is very soul destroying, it spoils the spirits inner wealth and in time spoils the outer wealth of life, even if the financial rewards are good, they are only good for a time, for wealth can become worthless if the soul is despondent or the days of life unhappy.

Once you decide to go into business, you need to know if you are better going it alone or taking a business partner.

If the ruler of your seventh house is retrograde, you can do much better in partnership, because the partner can bring out you latent business potential.

If you have Cancer on the tenth, seventh or as your zodiac sign. The right business partner will be a great help and support to you. Gemini too in these places is happier with a partner to help make decisions and to help sustain efforts. Anyone with a planet in the tenth house is generally better with a business partner so long as the partner is one described by that planet. Such a person can take your business and really raise it to the heights.

The ruler of the sixth or tenth house, in good aspect to the ruler of the seventh, or in good aspect to the cusp of the seventh house then a business partner is recommended as he or she will improve your success. And may have something of value to add to the business. If these planets are also in good aspect to the ruling planet of your eighth house, the partner may add capital to the business.

The Part of Fortune, in your first house, and trine to the midhaven, and you will do very well in self employment and on your own account. The first house is the self, the person life, and personal efforts. The midhaven is the career, The Part of fortune is where you'll make your " fortune" in life. Rather than from employment. You will become a self made person, with your "fortune" or fate in your own hands. This doesn't necessarily mean millionaire status, but it generally means you'll do well. You'll make your living and a comfortable one at that.

Ruler of your second house in your tenth, you will have to work for your money. It won't come from luck, or inheritance, and without any of the other signs, it won't come from a business partner either. This doesn't mean you shouldn't have one though. You may do equally well with or without a partner. IF the proposed partners chart is better than you, you may even befit form his luck or good fortune, but will still have to work hard.

Ruler of the tenth house in the first you may become a self made person. Your success will probably come to you before any subsequent partnership happens. The same if visa-versa and the ruler of your first is in your tenth. You will already be successful on your own account, before you take a partner, if at all. And your partner likewise will probably be doing well without you! That is not say you cannot do better together. But your first success will come alone and of your own solitary effort

The ruler of the tenth and ruler of first in mutual reception, you will prosper in business best alone.

What about adverse partnerships? Partnerships that can spell your ruination instead of success. These can show too., If the ruler of your house of money was in your seventh house at birth it is not a conducive sign to honest or advantageous partnerships and more so if the planet is negatively placed, or beset by bad aspects. Traditionally this means you can loss money in business through business partners or money in marriage through marriage partners, through theft, embezzlement misappropriation and fraud,. Taking that into account, if you have such aspects you would actually do better on your own than in partnership.

Neptune in or aspecting the seventh house is also a warning that partners may become deceptive or dishonest. May have their fingers in the cash box, or misappropriate stock or money and be good at concealing their thefts. The more so if Pisces is on the tenth or second house cusp. Take Saturn into account in a similar way. Saturn doesn't mean a light fingered partner far from it, Saturn is dedication personified, but Saturn can represent a person who may become treacherous and metaphorically may stab you in the back for his or her own advantage.

Ruler of the eighth or second house in your seventh house, a partnership with your husband, wife soul mate, will do well, alternatively you may marry money! When the ruler of eighth or second fall in the fifth house, it means the same as in the seventh, but also if appropriate to your age and circumstance, a business partnership with a son or daughter, or being employed by your son or daughter, would be advantageous to you. If these planets fall in the third or ninth house, a successful partnership with your siblings or uncles and cousins. In the fourth or tenth, with a former boss, or with your mother, father or step parent.

Ruler of your second house in your ninth look to a foreign or overseas partner. Consider an international business or one that has links abroad, export, import, foreign clients and so on.

If most of your planets fall in the eastern hemisphere of the horoscope, you are self reliant, independent and a self started in business. If the reverse is true and planets fall in the west, then you are better off as an employee, working for others, more than in partnerships.

Marrying money

Will my future marriage partner be well off?

To find out, take the ruler or lord of the eighth house (which symbolises partners money) If he receives good aspects from the Moon, Jupiter, Venus, Sun, or part of fortune. Then you will marry a wealthier man or woman. The closer the good aspect, e. g. conjunction and the closer the orb of the aspect, the wealthier your sweet predestined love will be.

Another old astrological law is If these same planets, or the north nodes, tenant the eighth house and are unafflicted, or if they rule the eighth. The partner will be wealthier than you.

If the ruler of the eighth and ruler of the second are in mutual reception (i. e. in each others houses and signs). The partner will be the wealthier

The ruler of the fourth or tenth, in good aspect to the ruler of the seventh from the angles, then he will have a good property or estates. Or a good inheritance to come.

But if the lord of the eighth is receives aspects from bad or malefic planets, then the partner is poorer than the self.

The karma of Money.

Many people's lives are out of balance, financially emotionally and in other ways. If you are indebted to others, if you owe anyone something, emotionally, financially or materially, if you don't pay those debts, (like doing a kindness in return for a kindness, though not necessarily to the same person who did you the kindness). The immeasurable balance is thrown out of order it becomes weighted more heavily on one side than the other, and over the years the weight increases, gradually others wont repay your kindnesses, wont do you good turns, wont loan you money. Life and money with it, will become emotionally and physically impoverished and will deteriorate. You could say the b very thought patterns that hem people into poverty are the end result of an upset balance. So part of the secret is in righting the karmic balance in life generally and then the money balance will also automatically begin to come right. All things are connected, even when we cannot see the fastening and hooks that hold the fabric of life together, they connect in subtle way, We have a collective karma and an individual karma.

What one person obtains for free, and doesn't pay for, other people have to pay for. There is no such thing as a free lunch, as the saying goes. But there is such a thing as having a lunch at someone else's expense and many people do it. At the time of writing in the UK, large coffee shop corporations and café chains and other gargantuan concerns are not paying their fair share of tax, the discrepancy is made up by the people having to pay the tax for then. The poor pay for the rich. People whose children get free education, travel, free school fool, and so on are subsidized be people who don't have children, as well as those who do, the world is full of inequalities. Those who travel free on the bus may take it for granted they should get free, just as parents take it for granted their children will be educated. There are no moral wrongs and rights about this, so let's not cloud the issue with debate. Part of the world's population is always supporting the other part. At times you will be the supporter at times the supported. Your free television channels and magazines are paid for by the advertisers I once heard it said if your don't watch the adds your stealing the programs. Nothing is free. Someone always pays.

This is the way of collective financial karma, we cannot know for certain that bus fares would be cheaper, if everyone had to pay the fare, or if. The busses and trains would still run, but emptier, if devoid of those whose seat is free But higher fare generally mean fewer people paying it, unprofitable buss roots are discontinued. When the bus stops running, it stops running for all,. It stops for the free travelers too Do not mistake my point, neither I nor any one else I hope, would want to see their grandmother struggle miles on her arthritic feet every time she visited a friend, simply because that state did not pay her fare, or give her enough pension to pay her own. No wealthy country would want to see a poor country dwindle and its people die out, or watch members of its own society suffer needlessly, and no one likes to see waste. Empty seats on a train should be used. The collective karma is not always within our control, but the collective is only a number of individuals, just as you and I. If you want to increase your own wealth there is the foot print of your own personal karmic debt and credit balance to consider amid all this..

We all have a karma of debt of some sort. Good things turn bad through debt, like the example of free transport that ends closed buss routes, our personal as well as collective debt can spread like ripples in a stream in ways that we would never wanted to happen. The old saying that tall oaks from tiny acorns grow is never truer. There is collective debt and personal debt. What is owed by you is being paid for by someone else somewhere, that is always a fact. If you owe people a kind word or a compliment, the kind word or compliment you are keeping to yourself and withholding is being paid for by someone who needs it, who is feeling that life is very cruel, it is being paid for by that persons suffering. A kind word can stop a suicide, A cruel word can be the last straw, all widening ripples in the pond that we may never see the result of it. The compliment that you owe someone, because you've been carping and criticizing at them more than they deserve is just as much a bad debt as what you own on your bank card and it, is being paid for by that persons suffering and drop in self esteem. Being conscious of Karma, means thinking what you owe, and also what you are owed.

The things you owe, are all debts of various sorts, money and, other kinds of debt are paid for by suffering worry, anger or the distress to people around you. The collective and the individual. The worry you cause your family, or the worry they cause to you is a debt. All the important things you get without paying for, other than gifts given with love, or given freely with an open heart without expectation of reciprocation, all the things that you take for free,, all the parasitic acts, all the things that are leeched from others, borrowed or begged in various ways they place you under a karmic debt. They load the balance far too heavily on one side, so that eventually any increase in your circumstance stops. If you always take but never give, if you're a boss who works your workers to death, if you bleed your friends and family dry. If you never work for all you could, if someone else always foots the bill for you, pays the price for you and your actions, and you give nothing back, you never repay. If you contribute nothing in any form to society and take all. The karmic balance of debts becomes turned against you, so in the end nothing more is given. Debts will be recalled, judgement day will come in your own lifetime. But there is the way to alter this.

To maintain good karma and a make a good future fate, a wealthier fate or to increase in all things from happiness to money, you have to give or put back something in equal balance for what you take in life, it all has to balance. If a person can understand this deeply, then they can sometimes act to improve their karma of debt, and rebalance their life. Awareness is the first step.

People cannot always pay their way financially, but that doesn't have to mean karmic debt as well as financial ones. If you give freely of things you have, including time, talent, the intangible things we all own, we contribute in other ways, pay the debt in other ways, your karmic debt balance and your life will always improve. Do not take things for granted, awareness is the first cornerstone to make this work. Most people take the freedoms of welfare and modern society for granted. The milk still comes from the cow, it wasn't made in a bottle or carton, somewhere far away form you in a barn or field there is a cow. If you cannot or will not work for your weekly money, then someone else is working harder than they need to, to earn you your welfare benefit for you., it didn't fall from the sky.

You have to think things through to their source. Someone is working to help you. They are working to subsidize you. They may feel it is for the common good an morally right to do so, or they may begrudge it to you under the doctrine of what is mine is mine, but that is not your karmic concern., such notions, along with feeling with guilt or feelings of entitlement cloud the karmic issue. The only facts that count are that you are getting something you haven't paid for. You may think you pay the cost in other ways, atoning with your current hardships, or suffering the slings and slights of unkind people who comment. You may feel your paying by never having any money or well being or not having the standard of life others take for granted But that's not payment it's self pity. Paying by misery is not the same as canceling out the karmic debt!.

You have to turn the balance round to make it a positive force in your life. That karmic debt to the unknown person, or anonymous crowd of supporting strangers will keep on accruing until you do. You have to have to take your equal share of giving back and contributing something to others if you want your circumstance to improve. This is one of the basic occult laws of karma.

Setting the balance of money karma right doesn't always mean having to equalize it correctly or exactly with money or with employment, which may be impossible at times. But it does mean scrupulously being conscious off it and setting in right other ways as soon as you can, If you balance your karmic debts so that you owe nothing, it is like balancing your financial debts, but your actual very real solid life circumstance will gradually change as if you have slipped into a different path, into a better fate or better karma coming into your life, good events will happen. The debt will reduce.

Money and karma are never separate.

There is also your karmic credits never forget those,, the ability to take, or demand what you are truly owed from life. Your inner self, your soul's depth knows what it is owed. Your surface self may be blinded by self pity, false pride, greed, idleness, it may think your owed things that are not due to you at all, but your soul truly knows the balance and can call on it.

Astrologically financial debtors charts, often have Neptune, the planet of waste and sacrifice, or the Moon planet of flux, or Saturn, hardship, in or aspecting the second house. Pluto aspects to the second can also warn of bankruptcy or severe crisis in fortunes at some stage in life. The period of bad debts and devastation usually begins when such natal planets become aspected by a malefic transit.

The second - eighth house axis of the chart shows the karma of money and the type of financial environment into which the soul accepts to incarnate. Heavy planets such as Saturn or Pluto indicate difficult karma, easy planets Jupiter Venus show the soul needs good financial conditions t fulfill the karmic purpose, or at least it needs not to be hindered by bad ones. When the Sun or Moon is in these houses the karma of money is old and deep. The Luna nodes show the karma of money is old and deep, and wealth is difficult to obtain, due to bad inheritance or conditions that existed before ones birth.

In some past lives money karma has to do with self worth and self confidence. The person who commands a high price for himself, his skills, values himself, but if he was not able to do so in past incarnations he may be born with self worth issues in this life that will again hinder what he try's for.

In other past lives the karma has to do with karmic debts. Retribution, if you have been responsible for another individual financial down fall in past life, it may be difficult to make head way in this, not due to punishment, but due to the soul having to be brought to understand the true consequence of their action, which can only be done by walking life in the victims shoes. When the lessons are learn such karma end s and the person is free to obtain wealth.

Karmic balance, the person who gives too much to others, the person who doesn't give enough. The settings can influence the present life karma.

Learning the value of money, very few people know the true value of money.

There are many other kinds of financial karma from our past lives that reflect in this one. So in working on oneself and ones karma, you are working towards wealth is spiritual way.

Water signs;

The Sun is weak and watery and reflective in the signs of Pisces, Scorpio and Cancer, tending to dreams, musings and inactivity. Solid wealth can take longer to accrue. The karmic lessons that these signs learn in the process of becoming wealthy is be to be realistic about money and work. These lessons may be difficult. Don't be inert waiting to be given things by luck or circumstance or people, will slow and depress everything. Action and assertion is required. Self- worth, confidence or lack of it, feelings of rejection by the world, the self or by others can be an intrinsic karmic element in the life of water signs. Possessions, gaining independence and wealth increase the self worth and confidence of these signs. So does finding a purpose or a lifeswork that one is cut out to do in life, and the wealth obtained from it be it financial or spiritual or both becomes a means of expressing the inner self. Values are important karma to water signs, including the most difficult value of all, learning to value, love and honour the self

The astrological karma of money is a vast subject and not really separate from other forms of karma, it is one piece of the jigsaw. But I have decided to include this fraction in the money book without making lengthy explanations about karma, reincarnation and the astrology of karma for it is money the book concerns itself with.

The latch Key to the Money in Your Chart.

Some people make money through their talent. Others through property, marriage, luck or employment. Once you identify which areas of your chart is a money box, and which is a poverty pocket. you can put more effort or direction into opening that money box and brining out the potential or good area of life. You can stop wasting efforts on false starts, and can also put your mind to changing or bypassing the bad areas of your money chart.

Jupiter is a giver of wealth. Saturn a restrictor. These two planets give you two directions to improve your wealth. Someone with say Saturn in the fourth house. House of the home environment, or first house, and Jupiter in the ninth, may find that they never have had much wealth or good prospects in their home town. Their beginnings may have seemed bleak and their hopes of better things blighted there. This is because Saturn represents limitations, he is conductive to poverty, the fourth house is the home, or home town. The " old" environments of ones roots. The signs of these houses will tell us more about the nature of the restriction. We could if we wanted build up a detailed picture of both the home town, its atmosphere, it's financial and emotional effect on the person. We could describe his actual home. But let's stick with this basic aspect. It points out a potential dearth of wealth, and pocket of hardship, or at least if not hardship then a dismastment of potential for better things. But a wider world is shown by Jupiter in the ninth house. This wider word may have more to offer. Such a charts owner would do well working or studying away from the home town, there would be less to hold him back, or if it were not possible or desirable for the person to move away physically to work or study, or to leave his background locality, then trying to reach an audience, customers, a trade, far outside his home town by other means, for example phone or internet, import, export, contacts with distant places and people would help his success.

A person with Saturn in the second or seventh house, cannot expect to gain a meal ticket or a millionaire by marriage! They may at sometime have to support the partner, this is their area of restriction. Or they be late in life finding a love and suffer the restriction of absences. If it is not possible to make the partner earn more money or work harder, or not possible to meet a partner sooner or at all, then Jupiter in the chart will show the best way they can improve their wealth if he is in the fourth they may find that their home and property is the asset to capitalize on, or in the tenth it will be the career. Saturn is lack. Jupiter is gain. Saturn is burden. Jupiter is ease. They are the twin of darkness and the twin of light. The double yoke in a chart, the two oxen pulling in different directions, which you can harness and make work for you.

The two planets need to be read together, yoked together to find what holds you back and what can take you forwards. I won't list all the Saturn Jupiter house combinations because. they are easy enough for you to work out for yourself, now that I have given you the key

If Saturn the planet of limitation, forms an opposition to Jupiter, by birth or by transit. Jupiter is the planet of plenty. Saturn the planet of shortage. The conflict between these two planets will accelerate the decline of money in your life. No sooner will you amass it than it will diminish. You want to move forward in your life, further towards your goals, but there will never seem to be enough money. You meet financial obstacles and resistance no matter how hard you try. At times a loss of patience, dashed hope and depression will pervade you. You would be wiser to reassess your direction in life under this aspect. You may discover, probably at a significant point in Saturn's or Jupiter's revolution, that you have been on the wrong track, most of your life, or you may discover valuable new insights about your current goals and purpose. There is a need to be more practical about money and your life's goals when these two oppose. When they conjunct, and so share the same house, life and trying to get money can be like a road of obstacles, it can feel like two steps backwards for every step forward.

The actual house they occupy will hold the biggest clue to its resolution. In the twelfth house for example, you are your own worst enemy, Or deepening on the sign on the twelfth house, things like secrets, institutions, prisons, past history, hold you back. In the ninth everything previous said of Jupiter there will hold true, but Saturn will incline you to choose the wrong place, or for there to be some impassible obstacles there, or you may simply not like being there.

Money and inheritance

The eighth house, as most of you will know is the house of death and inheritance. Any wills, heirlooms or legacy's left to you crop up here. Also this the house of your partners money, divorce settlements, taxation, death duties, insurances, all show in the eighth and by it's rulers, and aspects. Legacies are not always financial, as this anecdote about Chiron shows

Chiron in the eighth house.

The planet Chiron here means the parent may have had debts and poverty or was often borrowing money. A hidden ancestry of richer relatives, that may be known of unknown to you. A strange inheritance, an unfair situation around an inheritance, or a lost inheritance.

One client with Chiron in the eighth house, grew up with a fascinating mystery. He was born illegitimate, but to a wonderful woman. His mother adored him, she had a difficult life and for as long a she could remember she had taken solace in drink, but had never allowed him to become neglected or damaged by that in any way, or by his illegitimacy. He had her complete devotion, and attention and a life of fun, frivolity and companionship. She gave him whatever she could, she entertained him with stories and games, and his school friends were always wellcome and fed cake and tea, at her home. Over the years he had more than a couple of step fathers, who never lasted long but who while they were there served as the male influence in his life. Taking him boating and to watch foot ball and they were never allowed to chastise him or be unpleasant in the home. If his mother fought or quarreled with them, they were out on their elbow.

He did not miss having a steady father But he was curious. He had been told tales about his biological father, He was uncertain whether his "unknown" father was a high up titled lord, or whether this rumour was just one of his mothers drink induced fantasy's, one of her fairy tales, as he called them. She only ever talked of his father when inebriated and what other people told him was as much superstition, scraps or rumours which may originally have come from his mother too, or may not have. One morsel of the inheritance was that she had given him the same impressive forename as the lords, and the name " Lord" for a middle name, like some shred of identity and then her own sir name, and it sounded good. I cannot give his real name, so let's call him Damien Lord Frank. Chiron in this house can be a karmic challenge to salvage or reclaim something of the lost family fortunes. The ancestral line is important in some way. Though not always in the way one expects, and what is reclaimed is not always what one hopes.

His mother was an ostentatious colorful, woman, a semi alcoholic, who had spent time in a mental ward. She usually wore a large fur collar, a big hat with a floppy brim and had a small red dog that resembled a Chin, or a very tiny Spaniel, or one of the china mantelpiece dogs one sees for sale in English antique markets. The dog was tucked under her arm, she usualy had a Volumous patchwork handbag and a desire to be special. And she enchanted everyone she met. He, Damien lord Frank was an average boy. He didn't embrace any weird fashions, he left school without any grades, began work in a supermarket filling shelves, and then got a job in a bar. After several stages and as many years he himself became the licensee in charge of a local public house and he did well. He did very well and he was happy, as he had always been. But what of the lost inheritance, or Chiron's influence.

You could say he recouped not the Lordly fortunes but the money his mother had drunk down the years! and more. Which is a kind of reclamation of lost family fortunes. He said if his pub hadn't already had a name, he'd have called it "The lost lord" in honour to his mother, and the way she had made him feel special all his life. To an underprivileged and illegitimate child in England in the early 1960s when illegitimacy was still a stigma, feeling special when every other school boy in class but him had a dad, and more pocket money, and a bike, and the other trappings of an affluent childhood, was wealth indeed. He was also never bullied at school, many illegitimate children were in those days, but because his mother alcoholic as she was so charming and nice and welcoming to all his classmates He had a good life. The pub name would have been a fitting tribute, and another way of Chiron's ability to make the family line important. Chiron is also the way in which we are different and Damien's ancestry, his mother, even his illegitimacy, his name, which as not inherited in his case, but names usually are inherited, and his actual inheritance, His mother left nothing behind her, shed drunk it all. All this was different to that of his friends.

The karma of wealth or legacy from ancestry, is not always financial wealth. But if you have Chiron, or Neptune in the eighth house, or ruling it, and making a strong financial aspect in the chart, there is just a chance there may be a lost legacy there for you somewhere.

Now let's look at the other planets in the eighth house with regard purely to financial legacies.

Jupiter in the eighth, often means a financial inheritance. Transit Jupiter will also bestow a legacy. Neptune will loose one for you. Mercury will make it tricky to get your hands on it. Uranus will hammer you with taxations.

If the ruler of the eighth is in the twelfth house, the inheritance will be difficult to obtain, lost, hidden, obscured. Theft of inheritance. The sort of thing where you know Aunt Freda had cash or valuable jewelry in the house, but it mysterious disappears after her funeral and death. Where Mercury or Mars is involved relatives may misappropriate money. Neptune can also be deception, or mental illness, the wandering machinations of the elderly person mind that have placed the bank books in an inappropriate place or through some twisted notion, decided to deprive the inheritor The Moon can also point to feeble or frail mentality. When looking at transits, the moves too quickly to be counted in this way, but the Moon by progression to this house can make the inheritance doubtful or doubted.

An interesting chart

This is the chart of an inheritance; Sara was an only and illegitimate child, born to an obscure mother who lived in poverty, against a background of peculiar wealth. She grew up without knowledge of her true origins. Her mother was her father's mistress. Sara called her father "Uncle". This is what she was brought up to do, and she believed him to be her uncle. Her childhood was a tightly woven basket of deceit, laced with deliberate lies. Uncle Francis was always "kind" He paid for her boarding school education. Consequently much as she loved the school, she was rarely at home to know the truth. The house she and her mother lived in, had one rickety old table, one chair each, no carpets, a bed each and one cupboard that had come from some more industrial place. Only the basics. given by uncle Francis. He said this was all a person needed. A world of contrasts, the privileged private girl's school and the bare house Yet Sarah never questioned it.

Sara's mother like most women in England, at her time in history had no employment of her own, and suffered a stigma for being a lone woman with a child. Sara's was taught that her father was a dead war hero, who was little spoken of.. Pregnancy was an act of passion and death prevented the marriage. This was what Sara had been lead to believe. It's what she trotted out to her friends. At home the matter was never mentioned and Sarah did not question it, or ask anything more about her Father.

When uncle Francis visited, Sarah was sent out to play. He and the mother often had furious and thunderous rows. Sarah would listen at the door, it didn't intimidate or upset her at all. It mustn't have disturbed her mother either because the relationship as lovers continued unto death. Uncle Francis. lived a double life. He was wealthy, well known, possibly titled, and of course married.

He financed Sarah's education. He bought her a pony. He was to her the generous favorite uncle. The only uncle. The house remained frugal, neglected, but perhaps Sarah's mother did question that, or ask more. Sarah was a confident, happy, bold child. Kind and decent she made lots of life long friends at the school, finished her education and went abroad to work.

When Sara was in her early twenties, she was recalled home by her aunt, her mother who had been ill for some time by then and who had been very frail on Sarah's last extended visit was dying of cancer. Sarah remained with her. It was also the last time she was to see Uncles Frances. She buried her mother. Within a week of the funeral her father " Uncle Francis", had a major stroke, and died three days after.. It was only then that amid Sara's distress and devastation she uncovered the castle of lies, constructed so carefully over the years and found the truth of her upbringings. He died without legitimate issue, no children to his marriage. After a lengthy and considerable legal battle with his relatives Sara inherited a good part of a fortune. Enough invested money to pay her an annual allowance, that meant she didn't have to work, could afford the best house and car, and luxurious things she had long wanted.

Let's look at how the inheritance shows in the chart.

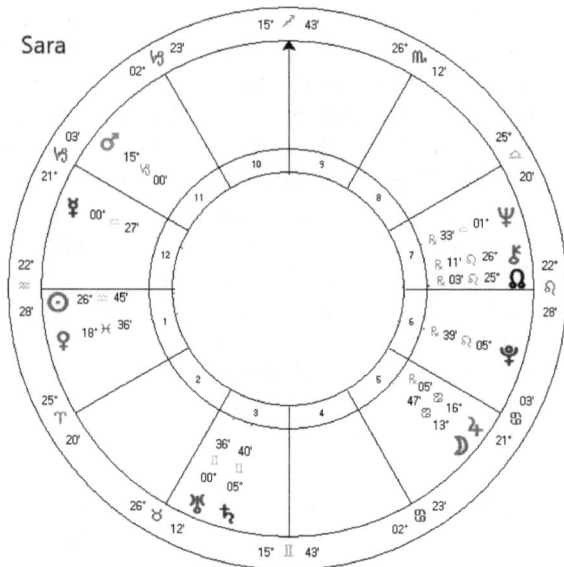

Sara

The eighth house being empty shows no previous expectation of any inheritance. The first clue is that the Sun, which represents the self, aspect the cusp of the eighth, showing inheritance, Venus ruler of the 8th is also in the first, linking inheritance with the self.

The father's house is ruled by Jupiter. At birth he was conjunct the Moon, showing a prominent father. Jupiter often equates with wealth, the Moon with fame. Her father was a well known wealthy man locally. Opposing Jupiter and the Moon is Mars, this aspect Moon Mars, Jupiter reveals the violent rows Sara recalled between her mother and father and later the legal fight she would have to obtain her inheritance. Remember that planets in the natal chart have different meanings at different times in life. But Mars is also Sara's money ruler, he rules the second. Showing a financial inheritance the legacy from her father. The ruler of the fourth house, home, mother, being in the twelfth, secrets trickery and deceptions and about childhood.

The Luna nodes across the ascendant and descendant linking Sun. Chiron shows a karma and crisis to do with her birth, and later her identity. Chiron like Jupiter both retrograde, truth and lies and things not revealed clearly until later in life.

Sara's second, house, and eighth house, tenth are empty and her chart does not show much potential to rise to successes on her own. She has Jupiter in the fifth, traditionally wealth through luck or good fortune. The death of her father cannot be regarded as fortunate, it was an even greater misfortune in that along with the grief and sorrows of losing him, and it opened the can of worms regarding old family secrets, illegitimacy, and a battle for her inheritance. But it was " good fortune" in the sense that if her father had been a poor man, there would still have been the same deception. loss and sorrow in the end, but no life long income to reclaim.

How to maximize your wealth

If you have a strong eighth house, try to envisage how this direction can be better brought into your life. The eighth house may be the house of inheritance but if you wait for people to die you'll wait forever! So we must look at this house of inheritance in another way too. A person in the legal professions for example, might find they gain greater success and wealth from specializing in wills, inheritances, then estates of the deceased. A nurse with planets in this house may find she gains more money while working in a terminal ward, or more in a hospice than she does in an outpatient's clinic. An assistant in a food shop would do best on the fish or meat counter. The wage may be the same, but the opportunities and fate that follows such a move are not, not if you have a strong eighth house. You will gain.

People who benefit form working with history in any way (i.e. our collectivize ancestry) may have a strong eighth house. So do those who work with the souls of the dead. The gain may not be directly linked to the change you make, the change is it is rather like steering a ship towards the port. It points your fate in the right direction, for other beneficial change to take place.

There are also with the eighth house strong, often wealth gained or money saved by recycling, reclaiming and reusing everyday things. Second hand goods. Transformed or restored or renovated goods. Antiques. Dead manuscripts, Old houses, collections of things that become valuable for the self or posterity, anything handed down to the future, be it a legacy or someone's old clothing.

The eighth is also money saved or gained by repair of items. Working in such an industry or business that closely approximates the one you are, in but adds an eighth house element and so directs you towards its natural path of wealth. Karmic rewards and karmic debts are also being experienced financially and in material things from earlier lives. So with the eighth house, which symbolizes death and rebirth and karma, in many different ways there may seem times when there is a strong fate but you have little control over the financial losses and gains in life. Everything you do to make the eighth house work better will improve your life.

If the eighth house is not especially strong or tenanted in your chart, then look to the house that is, and work in a similar way using the things it represents.

Muck and money

Psychologically as every Freudian knows there appears to be a forgotten tie between money and muck and various body orifices and parts. At the time of writing, money that is earned in a bad way is often called " Dirty Money". There is "Money laundering " the criminal act of making illegal or illegitimate money, go through channels and processes to make it appear correct or clean. There is blood money. Dough. Bread. Filthy Lucre. Putting ones money where ones mouth is. There is being " showered" with gifts from a wealthy partner. Money down the toilet, or money down the drain. The sink Where there is muck there's money, Popular slang and old phrases about money and filth and food and water encapsulate the subconscious Freudian oral and anal connection.

Money is sustenance, security, comfort. Money is the main provider when we grow up and leave the family and become independent and responsible for our self. Some people have a psychological problem with the transition and it can make them poor. The insidious squandering of money, disproportionate to what one has earned for support, or being an uncontrollable spender, a "shopaholic", is a psychological problem similar to comfort, or binge eating. Again the mouth the money. The disproportionate self denial of money, and the living meanly or in poverty and deprivation while one has a vast amount in the bank, is a psychological manifestation, similar psychologically to anorexia, and self starvation. The mouth the money. They are two sides of the same coin. This problem will make you poor and reduce your quality of life if you don't address it and resolve it.

In Freudian terms an anal or oral link. The eighth house is the house of elimination and purging in astrology, the second house the house of intake, or of feeding. If you have "comfort spending" or Shopaholic problems, Or problems related to self denial and miserliness, these are the houses to analyze first psychologically in your chart. Psychological problems of this type. Saturn which is associate more with self denial and financial starvation, wasting money away, meanness and leanness and with withholding money form the self. Jupiter or Neptune with binge spending, wasting away of money, and wasteful appetite for new things. Uranus can fluctuate between the two states.

Anorexics, like chronic misers, have a problem with "self worth", Anorexics deny themselves food, the very substance to maintain life, because fate or something or someone is denying them a life, or the right to have their own life, and maintain their own life as they want it to be. The miser denies himself money. Both the anorexic and miser have a fear of the future, of not having enough money or power to have the control to make things the way they want in life. Fear and having no other power to steer ones own life in the desired direction is a seed of destruction.

The body hate of the anorexic reflects how the soul feels. If he feels unacceptable to himself, he feels, ugly, sprawling fat, piggish. The inner and out image, of what life and what he is, is and what he could be instead, don't match up. He tries to sculpt the outside to match the inside. Anorexia is a slow form of suicide, slow because it's therapeutic, it hopes somewhere long the line, that it can transform the body to the thin and lovable self that might be worth more, the life rebuilt and sculpted into a better life. It hopes it can find a life worth living. Anorexia is a both problem and a solution. An alcoholic once said to me " Drink is not my problem, it's my solution". Wise words. You cannot solve a drink or eating problem without solving the life problem that caused it. This book is not about Anorexia or Alcohol, it's about money. Unnecessary money starvation when you can afford to live well, is also an issue about self worth and it's a self abuse. It is about deprivation, self denial, about living meagerly and being cruelly denied or excluded from the life you deserve and could have instead.

Ask these questions of yourself. What is so worthless about you that you cannot even spend your own money on you? Who was the first person in your life to make you feel that way, to *unnecessarily* deny you money? The first one to make you feel you weren't worth giving money or valuable things to, or spending on? " Who first made you feel guilty about every penny spent on the self? Who second? Who encouraged you to perpetuate this delusion, this lie about yourself who made you feel worthless? That you cost too much, that fine thing were not for you, who made you feel not good enough to spend money on, what circumstance made you feel, you had to go without because you weren't worth what you wanted to have ? or to go without so others could have? "These questions have clues to unraveling your past, to finding out who lied to you, and why even today, so many years on you still believe that cruel lie. For it is a destructive terrible lie unforgivable lie and, you are worth far more than the person who embedded it in your spirit. The spirit of a little child most likely who would be that cruel to a child. Doing this, self awareness exercise may help you overcome the rags of your self imposed frugality.

The miser to the spendthrift! The comfort eater, and comfort spenders, suffer the same problem, except they are psychologically " Giving" to themselves, because no one else will, or does, because they too have been denied a feeling of being essentially at the core of your being worth something, or being worthy of love and generosity. This is an unfilled need in your life, a subconscious hunger that can never be satisfied by food or spending, because that's not what's really craved. The spending is a symptom it's not the disease, that's why what bought won't remedy it. That why you have to have another spending spree soon after, just as a drug addict has to have another needle. It is an anodyne that alleviates the pain of reality.

Sometimes over spending is also a kind of self compensation, to help you cope with a bad time or difficult task in life, but then in the years after that time, it becomes habit forming. When was your first financial fling? When was the second? What was going on in another area of your life then ? Were you spending to see yourself through a hard time, or an insecure time in your life. A time when you needed to feel good, but didn't? When did you splash out to compensate or console yourself in your sorrow, loneliness, or misery? Who was the first person you wanted to give you love, understanding, time, attention in your life and not things? Who was the second? Who in your life now do you want that from but aren't getting it from?

Some of these patterns formed in the past may have been necessary or helpful at the time. Times when you had to go without or scrimp and scavenge every morsel, 'waste not want not' times. They may have seen you through a hard patch like a wooden staff of support, but they may not be necessary now. In which case they can be dismissed, left behind with the memories and wounds and debris of emotion, that lie like garlands of sea weed and the flotsam and jettison and pebbles on the tide line of life. Release these things and you free yourself. They no longer have a necessary place in your life. If you cannot release them, if they are no longer habit, but still needed to help you face life, then you have to work on the issues and circumstance that has been revealed about self worth, self compensation and so on, and resolve those, before you can leave it behind. The leaving behind is generally a process, a fading, it is seldom a sudden end to the self denials or spending sprees, it just happens less often until eventually it isn't a problem.

At a certain stage progress may stop you may get stuck and have to ask yourself the same questions again or explore the avenues that the answers have opened up, to achieve a further diminishment. When you finally leave this chapter of your life behind the spending and saving patterns in your life will normalize and this will allow you to become wealthier, as well as happier. Chart aspects to look for in self denial and compulsive saving or frugality are; Saturn in hard aspect to obsessive planets like Pluto, Astrologically compulsive spending, saving or any obsessive behaviour can be connected with Pluto and money planets. With compulsive spending patterns he may be aspecting or crossing the second house by transit. Jupiter may be involved by aspect. With wasting, spending or gambling, Jupiter sometimes Neptune are in obsessive aspects with Pluto. The Moon is often involved in the aspect somewhere, it can be more the complex chart patterns, or obsession, frugality or waste and mal adjustment, than specific aspects that are involved.

An Unfortunate Chart

Wayne is a twin, born into a large family of poverty. His mother who was ill with her nerves, lived on social welfare and in social housing, on a crumbling dilapidated estate. The father worked, but contributed very little. He was a cruel and violent man.

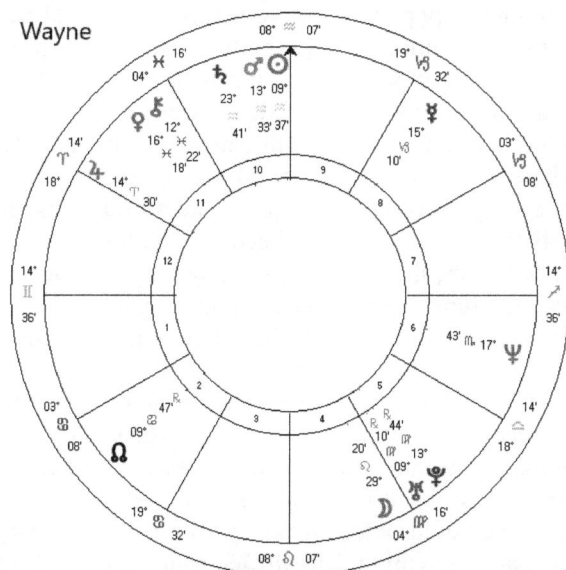

Wayne

The Luna nodes show wealth is difficult to obtain, due to a bad inheritance or conditions that existed before ones birth. Many wealthy people claim a difficult or poor beginning, it is fashionable to have come from nothing now and dragged oneself up by the boot laces. But their claims seldom stand up. Rich people have usually played at being poor at university. The really poor don't go to university. Wayne has the distinction of leaving school at sixteen and has never much worked since. To quote him "I went into school with nothing and I came out with nothing" Wayne gained no grades of any kind. He could be wise and philosophic. "The more I know, the less I know" He would say.

He was inventive in a practical way. His home circumstances were dismal. He made good use of discarded things, had mended his mattress, using a carpet sample. His dream was to be a multi millionaire pop star. But sometimes he would say "The more money I have the less I see the point of it". He is right of course, you can only drive one car at a time, only wear one coat at a time. This attitude is not as defeatist as it will sound to some people. There are people out there who make more money in a single second than some could spend or use in a lifetime. Money does become pointless after a certain sum, though that sum may vary for each of us, but most people have to have gain a *lot* of money before they learn that there is a point when the money doesn't matter.

His environment was discouraging and he seemed to lack the will to work. When work was perhaps the only way for him to rise out of it. Or perhaps he felt it was hopeless and that the kind of work he could obtain would not be enough money to change anything. The difficult inheritance of his mothers "nerves", has its part, for both Wayne and his twin suffer from chronic depression. The ruler of his Gemini ascent (Mercury,. mood swings) in the house of inheritance, in Saturn (depression) sign. His twin brother Jess was diagnosed with schizophrenia, but Wayne wasn't. Again the sinister inheritance, the old mythology that with two identical twins one is always born, odd, mad, or not right in some way. Jess life and character was not very different from Wayne's. Except Jess had the additional problem of his "voices". The enemy within and Jess when young had less ability to mix socially. Wayne was the more extrovert of the twins.

Over the years Jess the schizophrenic twin, has been Wayne's shadow and his burden. He has clung closer than an over coat. From school onwards, it automatically fell on Wayne's shoulders to take care of Jess. To look out for him to side with him, to always be with him, to provide him with constant companionship, to slide into Jess's strange perceptions of life and be part of it, this problems with reality, as Wayne called it. Wayne liked Jess's company, they were good friends as well siblings. He had little other company having to steer and buffet Jess though a hard world, He was avoided. No one wanted to risk the mad twin. So because Jess was always there, Wayne didn't make many new friends of his own. Living in the same house, same room, with no work or separate activity, Wayne could hardly be expected to find the way to keep his own life separate, his own friends, or his own sanity separate. This was not a choice he made, it was how life was. Given a choice he might not have changed it, but it has undoubtedly added to Wayne's own isolation and restricted him more than a shackle of iron.

Jess was much less employable. He couldn't have held down a job on his own, due to his unsociable and introversion on leaving school, which his the formative time for employment. Wayne might just have managed to do so. Had they both got a job together, Wayne could possibly have continued to carry him, they may have both benefited. But it wasn't forthcoming and so Wayne effectively was prevented by Jess's pervasive undermining influence to have a job himself. Psychologically Jess, did not want to face the world alone, and didn't want Wayne to be independent of him.

The years have insidiously sapped Wayne's confidence. Jess by the tragedy of his unintentional subtle dominant distorted mental day to day influence combined with the consolation of his loyal friendship and niceness. For Jess is a nice person. He is not the insane demonic twin of myth. They are both nice people. This and the subtle exclusion of other friends. Other doors in life, the complete insidious social isolation of poverty and unemployment was quietly devastating. Where one twin went the other twin went. What one twin thought, the other thought. A brotherly love that was both a blessing and burden to lonely Wayne, who couldn't envisage life without the company of his brother. Many the time, he said without Jess I would have no one. I wouldn't have a life. But equally he could not make new friends, or make any progress in any direction of life while he had his brother to carry.

Wayne's chart is difficult. The ruler of his twelfth house, house of sorrows and difficulties was in his house of career. It indicates Difficulty in finding employment. Jupiter the planet of prosperity was conjunct the twelfth house cusp, another difficult aspect. He also had Saturn, the eighth house ruler, in the house of Career. Poverty through the Career or in this case through lack of career, a dead career, and the influence of the difficult "inherited" burden and background. A hindrance or block in the ability to rise in life. since

Mercury, makes a quincunx to the ascendant From his Luna node axis we know there are karmic lesson for him to learn about money.

His Sun conjuncts his twelfth ruler, again indicative of a hard life, and this again in the house of career. Wayne dreamed of fame and exaggerated wealth, through music, he wanted to be a pop singer he talked of all the good he'd do with his future wealth. The old lady with the unofficial animal shelter, who given him his big chunky Labrador, the joy of both Wayne and Jess's life. He'd say he would build her a real animal sanctuary and pay for the animal's food and bedding. There was the deserted house he'd make good, for people like the homeless friend he met one day, who tramped the country. The things he would do for Jess, and his mother, who they lived with. The environment, the ducks in the park.

But he did nothing at all to bring this musical career about. He didn't join a group, he didn't find a venue to play. He didn't busk in the street, he didn't try and educate his musical skills more, or meet others in the music trade. He practiced in his room, he believed fame would walk up to his house and find him. That he didn't need job because fame would bring wealth in its wings (Neptune in the sixth house, square his tenth house planets, the great and driving delusion that made life worth living, but was an escape from pain, and fame remained elusive). I wished it had come to him, he was a lovely guy who would have made the world a better place.

Wayne had an abnormal dread of pressure from the department of employment, the attempts to find him work (Saturn in tenth fear of authority figures) and the threats to stop his welfare benefit and conscript him into various schemes. But he made no personal effort and took no interest in finding employment. He never tried to wrongfully gain extra benefits, or extra state help, or to swing-the-lead. It is possible he was entitled to much more than he claimed, for his fear of the benefits office prevented him making enquiries. He has become accustomed to his poverty and the restricted life that poverty enforces. If I could wish anyone some money it would be Wayne. I wouldn't wish him a pointless amount though I'm sure he'd do more good with it in the world than many who have vast fortunes. I'd wish him a nice amount, so he could have a few luxuries, retain his beautifull philosophy in life, and do a little bit of good for the animals and people was so fond of. That indeed is wealth. There is a different between having wealth and having money. Wayne is wise enough to know the difference.

Wayne is not so much living freely as building his own prison, taking the line of least resistance in what seems a heavy fate, instead of attempting to live through the chart it in a positive way that would bring him independence, greater wealth, and a sense of purpose. Saturn in the tenth house, always needs a sense of purpose. Wayne has denied himself that. He would say that music is his sense of purpose, but it is not so in his case, music is his escape, it is the illusion that prevents him seeing the walls of his prison. If music was his predestined purpose he would have done more to make the dream real., because that how a predestined or karmic purpose works. One way or another it finds it road. He'd have been playing and singing in a hotel, a pub or club, in the street. He'd have a life worth living, so that he would not need the dream.

Heed have taken a step on the path and the path would have taken a step to meet him. Part of his mind knows this, it's why he doesn't try to make it real, like an egg it could shatter too easily in his hands and leave him with nothing. His chart shows his musical talent but it also shows the enigma of his true vocation that would give real meaning and transformation to his life. It may lie in a different line of work altogether. The aspect is again a quincunx. A difficult transformation, but not impossible.

As we can see from the chart Both Pluto and Uranus aspect the tenth house planets, so there is the ability in this challenging chart to totally transform the utter poverty and perpetual unemployment and live life in a very different way. This is a daunting chart, you are probably expecting me to say that Wayne is now a multi-millionaire and to relate his climb to success, but I cannot cheer you by telling you the sequel to Wayne's story, it doesn't have a sequel.

It is an example of living through the chart in a negative shadowy way, As I have repeatedly said in this book, you can live through the negative side of your chart and have nothing, Like Wayne you can close your mind to wealth, or you can turn it around, work with it and live through the positive side, and fate will come to greet you with one arms of abundance and you can become rich beyond your dreams.

Truth and failure

Loss by failure.

The ghost of failure taps at our windows and howls in the darkness of the small hours of night. It can be a self destructive, failure that touches on the ragged edges of self worth and lack of it, tugging with horrid little icy fingers at the soul. There are two ways to regard failure. One is that failure and poverty, are all preludes to success. It is what comes after that is important,. not what went before. Don't make the mistake of thinking because you have failed in one venture, that it reflects the whole of your being, or existence, you are the same fine person now as before you failed in this thing, a little wounded perhaps, a little more damaged by life, but you have not become suddenly worthless, or stupid or foolish, or the pigs ear, simply because you did not succeed this time.

If you failed a hundred times you still would not be those things. You'd still have the ambition and courage to try and the visions and energy and effort and willingness to risk it all, You are not less of a person. do not let hurt pride and battered ego, or the judgement and misjudgment of others convince you otherwise or allow them to sap your self estimator prevent you from trying again. But equally do not make the exact the same mistakes again, or enter into some other venture prematurely on the rebound as it were. Do not lie to yourself that is equally as important as not blaming yourself. Excuses and lies are what we give to other people, the truth is for yourself. However good or bad you are you will not succeed unless you face up to who you really are.

Analyze accurately what when wrong, then move on. Learn, and begin again, or if you decide from your analysis it's better to discard or scarp this particular venture, do so, take a change of direction for your next venture.

Failure is due to many things, including chance and timing and things beyond your control, and how much money you have to begin with, for a wealthy person will always succeed better than a poor one, simply because he has the safety net of money behind him to help success. Numerous factors that can even include your age, sex, manner and appearance, when these things should have no bearing at all. But no delude yourself it is all circumstances or pure chance, bad luck, recession, incompetence of others or lack of a new shirt that made you fail, for in part it is also what you did wrong. Failure of a venture can be like failure of a relationship, whatever else want wrong or to was blame, There is still some blame to you, at the very least you did not choose the right person to love, if you had they would have still been with you. You assessed something wrongly. You may or may not have done other things. If you have analyzed correctly, without self delusion will see success next time. Never be too cruel to yourself. You will meet enough other hard cruel people on your way to success to last you a lifetime, I promise you that. So you don't need to do to yourself what other do to you.

Success is the best revenge. Keep this in mind, when you are angry. When people have made you feel small. You have the power to rise again, keep this in mind when you are defeated. Forgive people their transgressions if you can, if you cannot do not torment yourself with hate or anger, self pity. Tears or hopes. A mind that is cleared of these emotions, has no bitter seeds to grow and poison it. It has a clear path of destiny, a clear road to wealth.

Luck and attracting it.

Can good luck really be blocked by fate, or tied up like a knot in time. The question is how to loosen it? The inner soul always knows the means to unlock this situation, finding it is the first step. Undoing it the second. Increase your fortunes the third.

Some people believe that bad vibrations disrupt the potential for wealth. or form a barrier which blocks off all forms of good events linked to money or happiness which could change the course of your Destiny. The art of making talismans to offset such vibration is as old as time and requires special astrological as well as magical skills. But simple mailmen's can be made by drawing on the power of your chart to bring good luck. Wearing jewelry made of stones colors, and so on associate with your house of money, and combing them with your personal zodiac colors and gems.

When transit Jupiter conjuncts certain planets luck can come your way, when the planets are linked with money, say the second house ruler, the luck can be financial. The fifth house ruler, if luck is to come through gambling, the eighth if it is come through loans, other peoples money. Good aspects to the third and eighth or their rulers by Jupiter and say your ruling planet, if it is to come from a sibling or aunt or uncle, or is to do with education such as educational grants, scholarships and so on, Plotting your Jupiter transits can tell you the best time to gamble, the best time to clinch a deal, It will give you the edge. So will plotting the transit aspects of the ruling planet of your second house, It is also a good time to under Jupiter transits buy talismans for money, to work spells if you are interested in the occult and it's ways of gaining money. To say prayers.

There is the old and well known magical and religious formula that money needs to circulate to grow". That when ever you receive money, or a good gain you must send a little back into circulation, to keep the wheel of fortune turning in your direction, or in religion you give a Tithe. This formula is often elaborated on or ritualized individually, some people bless paper money before they spend it, and ask it to return speedily. Others give a tithe, or small amount or gift to some person who is appreciated, or to a deserving person, or charity when they have good luck. This tends to work when Jupiter is strong in the chart. Remembering also that money is only currency, so what you give back doesn't have to be money. There are many old formulas and " money spells" Candle spells, in Magic and occult books., But Our own instincts and personal superstitions usually show us a formula that will work for us, but it may not always work for others, because our spirit knows best what's in our chart and required to balance our own individual life. Someone with a strong Saturn will be different to a strong Jupiter. A strong Saturn accumulates be saving and conserving, not be circulating and tithing.

To help you gain money here is a list of the traditional lucky colors associated with planets and signs. The colour you must wear to attract money, should be chosen from the sign on your house of money, or your eighth house, which signifies other peoples influence on your money. If you have a planet in that house that colour should be included. If you want luck at a work interview, say a wage rise, include a colour or item from your sixth house,

house of work. In the case of Jewelry, keep sakes, items, precious and semi precious stones, carried for luck, buy only what your soul feels drawn to. If you see nothing in the colour that you like, wait until such a time when you do, for luck has to be drawn to you it's like love it cannot be forced.

Use this list or to choose in a "lucky item", for example a scarf to wear at a job interview. A pen, an ornament a trinket, a lucky stone, something symbolic of the wealth you want to win, or the use you intend to put the wealth. For gambling if your into horse racing a toy or ornamental horse for instance of the colour, or if you intend to win enough for a holiday something symbolic of the destination. The old magical law of like attracts like is linked to an old astrological law. But you must also be attracted to the thing you buy, that is another old occult rule that sets up the right vibration. The more you like the item, the more you bond with it and so bond with the like attracts like vibration of fate.

The colours

Leo or the Sun; yellow, lemon, gold metallic, and light orange tones. The colours of flame and of the Sun itself. Sandy, muddy shades, when mixed with other planet influences like Saturn or **Capricorn.** Gilt, brass, yellow metal come under Leo. When mixed with the Moon, very shiny and light reflecting yellows and growing whites.

Cancer or Moon; Whites, pearl shades. Light cream, Silver metallic, opalescent and oyster shades

Gemini or Mercury; light green, lime green (also fawns and fudge colors, pastel shades of brown- Mercury rules two signs you see, the green associated with Virgo, the fawn associated with Gemini)

Venus; pink, mauve, copper and bronze metallic. (the planet colors are symbolic, the reason Venus is pink, she is the planet of love and peace., Mars is passion, sex and also war, so he has red, colour of blood for war, but Venus being love is sexual passion (red) but diluted with purity, peace and spirit. (white, So she is shades of pink). Copper is the metal she rules, and so also anything coppery or bronze or autumn leaf.

Mars; Red, scarlet, crimsons, bright reds and darker blood reds. Carmines and vermilions.

Jupiter; blue, turquoise, sky blue. Azure, blue bells and violet's. Mauve and lilac.

Saturn; dark brown. woody brown, grey, slate grey, lead grey battleship grey. Ash colours. Black and almost black.

Neptune; dark green, and blue greens, streaky mingled greens. Colours of the sea or water, transparent ice colours, clear glass colours. Neptune rules fake and look alike items, like fake or imitation gold. So if you have good Sun- Neptune aspects to your second house, brass and yellow metal will be luckier than gold.

Pluto; black.

Uranus; Changeable colours, Dark purple blues. Dark lilac. (When Uranus was discovered, astrologers of the time wrote that he ruled mixed mingled colors, checks and plaids, tartans and this is true. But I think this was only because they did not have a spare colour for him. My own research and observation has re classified him as being purple, and shades of violet as this seems to work. But also I will include traditionally mingled colours, marbled colours, and rainbows.

The signs are basically the same colour as their ruling planet, as both possess the same vibration. Though astrologically the signs are regarded as weaker more diluted than the planet, as the planet is the concentrated strength or vibration of the sign, So a planet would be more intense in colour tone, than a sign, the sign is the same colour but paler, lighter, diluted, but basically the same colour, for example, Aries, is light red, while Mars darker intense vibrant red The list includes precious stones, metals and substances. That will help bring money and profit in your life. These things are well known, so much that they are often disregarded as not being serious astrology, but like zodiac signs they deserve some space in the book..

The Signs

Aries; the colour red, Red Jasper, Ruby, Garnets, red stones and pebbles. Iron, steel. Diamonds. Red Jade, also red glass. Zircon, Amethyst,. Heliotrope, All sparkling and fiery substances. Sapphires can also bring luck more so pink sapphire.

Taurus; orange, cream. Jade, emeralds, moss agate, coral, lapis lazuli. Carnelian. Howlite. Buttermilk Jasper. Cream coloured stones. Orange ambers. Carnelians. Gold stone. Orange calcite. Jewelry made of natural substances, including cloth and carved wood. Jewelry in the shape of animals. If you have the Moon or Venus in Taurus in aspect to your second house, lucky jewelry, scarves, enamels, and so on will have a plant or flower design.

Gemini; fawn, light toffee, buff, very light browns Jewelry made of two things together. Picture stone. Quarts crystals. Fluorite, beryl, chrisolite. Also veined substances, like marble. Modern, new and fashion jewelry.

Cancer; white and off whites, pastel tints that are whiter than anything. Mother of pearl. Opals, Moonstones, silver, platinum, opal, clear quarts, emerald, silvery substances. Family jewelry, Heirlooms, jewelry of a sentimental nature comes under this sign.

Leo; yellow, and whitish yellows, pale lemon. Brass, Gold, Azurite, and valuable jewelry. Golden or yellow ambers. Yellow jade. Personal jewelry and Jewelry of lasting value comes under the Sun.

Virgo; green, leaf greens and olive greens, muddy light browny greens, and the green colour almost between dark muddy yellow and green, Peridot, Light green ambers and jades. Aventurine, topaz, aqua marines, Green agate. Glass. Almandine,

Libra; pale pink, light pinks, candy pink, bubble gum pink. Decorative glass. Copper. Rose quartzes. Pink opal, cornelian, beryl, red gold, Nephrite, brass, colored glass and substances which reflect light or are highly polished. Jewelry associate with love and romance.

Scorpio; black. (ancient astrologers said red, because Pluto had not been discovered, and red does seem to work as a secondary or alternative to black for Scorpio) Malachite. Jett, Black glass Black onyx, Bohemian glass, Hematite, Topaz, red amber, all dark murky and mysterious substances. Meaningful and mystical or occult jewelry.

Sagittarius; blue, azure Wedgwood blue and grey blues Lapiz Lazuli. Sodalite. Beryl. Hezatite. Turquoise Blue lace agate. Amazonite, Blue john. Jewelry of religious significance. Jewelry of clubs, fraternities. Masonic jewelry

Capricorn; brown, earth brown and terracotta browns, bronzy brows and yellowy browns. Fossils. Amber. Jet, coal, lead pewter. Moss agate. Old, and second hand jewelry, Onyx, Sapphire, dark mottled substances. Amber, Ammonites, antique jewelry, though not necessarily valuable, and things of the past.

Aquarius; lilac and light purples, lavenders Amethyst. Azurite. Mystic quartz, may faceted cut reflective glass and crystal. Bohemian crystal. Alexandrite, sapphire, hematite, amber, slate, electric tones and magnetic substances. Antique jewelry and hand made arts and crafts items.

Pisces; pale green and white green and pale blue green

Items of glass, clear quartz, Sea glass. Serpentine, some light greenish and blue green jades. White gold, shell and coral. Aquamarine. Foreign, exotic and imported jewelry. Also religious jewelry.

Mars

Mars is the planet of jelousy, a negative Mars, Mars conjunct Chiron, Mars in the second house; can stop you obtaining wealth due to jelousy of others. Chiron can stop you obtaining wealth through a sense of injustice or unfairness.

To overcome bad Mars or Chiron karma locate the poison in your soul by finding the original thorn that tears into your flesh. Is it the injustice of your poverty ? Are you bitter at a unfair world, who makes others rich while you are poor, do you blame the person who has what you do not? Do you hate or envy him? Did it begin with jealousy of someone known to you, a wealthier or move fortunate sister or brother? Try to find the root so can overcome the root, or so that your subconscious can realties that was appropriate in the past is not helping anymore, so that the root can be abandoned and left behind you. You may have been envious of someone when you were young, but now you're not young so you have to put aside childish things. Begin by helping those who have less than you, to be equal to you, not by crying and railing at the injustice of those who have more. As this begins to set right a karma It makes you more equal, others more equal, and the message sent to you subconscious like sunlight going through a glass window, is that you are equal and more.

Action perpetuates action. Then by the mysterious force of life, after a time you will find this psychological pattern you have set in motion for yourself, soon means being equal and more to those who were once above you. If it is the injustice of equality and jealousy of those above, always try to make the world and your small part of it fairer more financially equal place. Then Try to remember the first time ever, maybe when you were a small child, the first time that springs to mind when you felt that same sense of unfairness or injustice in life. Look at that injustice again but with adult eyes. It may help untie a very old and personal psychological knot in your being and help this kind of karma loosen. The past and the present often have echoes of each other. Money and emotion have echoes, because money has to do with financial material survival, and emotions with. Psychological survival.

A thorn in the flesh is sometimes not only the injustice of someone having more than you, but rather the particular individual who has the wealth to which you feel more entitled. A hateful enemy; The favorite brother who got the inheritance that should have been yours; The unpleasant man who got the promotion and pay rise you deserved;, someone who hurt you or ridiculed you in the past, who's continued wealth and success is like galling like an open wound to you now. It may have been an utter stranger but of the very type of person you most detest who does that detested person, or situation remind you of? That is a key to ridding yourself of the knot, the issues you had with the other person, not the stranger. These negative emotions block your own path to wealth. The karma of such an emotion can bind you poverty until you unlock the trap of them. when you give up your hate and jelousy, the stored angers you will be rewarded with wealth.

We all know the world is unfair. The way to redress the balance is to work on the roots of your own grudging hates instead of dwelling on what the person has gained, when you understand how those roots have grown to strangle your spirit and untangle them from the misery you feel, you may free yourself enough from this blockage to gain wealth. To rid your self of this hate that is binding you to poverty, ask why do you hate the person for having money?, or do you only hate the injustice, the fact that you don't have it. Be clear about what the hate is, and that is a step closer to finding why you hate. If it's injustice or your own poverty you hate. Then hate that, not the other person who has what you don't, and that is one tiny step forwards. The next step, if it's injustice you hate, is to stop being unjust yourself, in all situations in your life, to make a point of being fair in all things. If it is jealousy, then counter it by thinking of yourself as equal as good as that person. Jealousy often has it cause in feelings of inferiority to another person, feeling less loved or less admired. Finding why you feel this peculiar inferiority will make you realise that we are all different but equal, what you give out, you get back.

If it's not the wealthy person you hate but your own poverty, begin by helping those worse off than you. This puts you in the shoes of the richer person. It may even make you better than there richer person your hatred is directed at, if they are not helper or givers, at the very least it will put you on their level but in a different way. Like attracts like. It trains the mind on a subtle level like a ritual. It may help you overcome your negativity that is standing in the way of your success.

Another hidden cause of this emotional negativity is sometimes sibling or peer rivalry, or jealousy that is at the root. The stranger you hate may remind you of someone else, for how can you hate someone you really don't know at all? Even if you know a few scraps about them, it is not enough to hate. Who do you really hate? Who do they remind you of? Subconscious jealously? A rival from childhood, a sibling, someone you were always jealous of but others admired? Or some part of your self you'd rather disown? The greed for the wealth they have may really be a disguised desire for what you hoped for in the past but did not get. The desire for love, approval, adulation you wanted then, the residue of which is still holding you back now. We have to make sure it's money or wealth we really want, and not the things that we associate with it, such as success, fame, freedom from responsibility's, otherwise we are barking up the wrong tree, and so will always be held back at the first step.

The process of removing the psychological blockages that are preventing greater wealth will give you two kinds of opulence, Money and a greater spiritual wealth that comes from the increased self awareness. Because one thing begins to echo the other in life. The spiritual and the material they are not separate. All things are connected.

Chart of a beggar

This curious chart belongs to a man who describes himself as having the eyes of a Yogi. Powerful eyes that both attract and frighten people. Vijay (VJ) is a fascinating and intelligent man with a wealth of weird experience. He was educated a Christian mission school, learned English there. He is well read, His intelligence and his literary grasp of the language are comparable to many of my public school clients. When I read VJ's first letter to me, I thought here is an oxford educated man. He was already in his seventies then.

The curious thing about VJ is that most of his life he has lived as a beggar on the streets of Singapore, and almost entirely on hand outs. His story is not tragic. He is a happy man, when it's cold, he rents a room. He has seen a side of life that few of us ever will. His letters were long and interesting and he insisted on paying for work I did for him. His chart at a glance with its fifth house Saturn, showing lack of good fortune, and lack of lucky chances. The twelfth house Sun, having to rise through darkness of difficulties in life, also possibly history to do with institutions.

His house of money, shows Neptune, this symbolizes his living made from begging., or idle ways. Also with Neptune in this house it is hard to accrue lasting wealth of nay kind. Venus is here on a cusp. He told me as a younger homeless man, he was often paid for his sexual services by women. This still happened occasionaly. He did not seek or commission this work. In more recent time tourists sometimes wanted to pose for a picture with him, and gave him money, because he managed to persuade them he was a kind of traveling Guru.

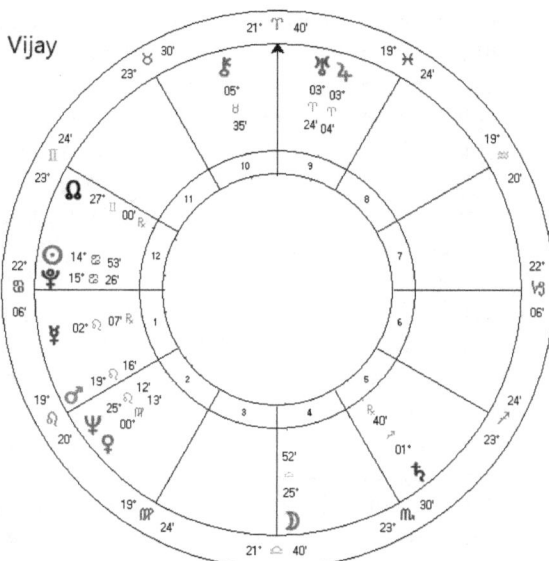

Vijay

This is his Neptune, Moon aspect. His fourth house Libra Moon, shows frequent changes of residence, shifting round from rented room to room, sometime renting a space in an alcove or passage instead of a room, but with a love of his home place, which he now regards as Singapore, and never traveling far from it now. Though he has traveled extensively in his younger years

Mars is like a mystery in his chart glued to the second house cusp, it would suggests one ambitious for money. And being ruler of the tenth we would expect a brilliant Career, One who was very good at his chosen profession. VJ is an excellent beggar. He told me he never went short of anything. Food, clothes, conversation, money, it is all provided by the world. But it is the experience of life and people he meets that interests VJ. He is a conversationalist, a correspondent, not money minded. None of his questions were ever about increasing his wealth, or work. Not all beggars are poor, some are very rich. some are confidence tricksters who trade on people's pity and make more in hand outs than the people who mistakenly give to them out of compassion. But VJ was not of that kind. He had too much pride to trade on people or pity, not with Mars in Leo. he was a princely beggar. He was not rich, but he got by. He had money to rent his post office box to collect his letters, money to pay his lodgings, though he sometimes liked the open the summer nights outside. Money to eat and wash. His true vocation as shown in his chart was that he should indeed have been a Holy man, and perhaps in his way he was. He had no fixed religion, he attended many churches and temples, because of the free food and coffee after the ceremonies. He liked all things religious, philosophical and psychic and mystic and astrological interest him.

Past life karmic influences

If wealth did not bring you happiness, love, or the things you really desired in a past life, or if you came to associate wealth with pain in former incarnations, then your spirit may secretly resist or turn away from wealth in this life. So that you hinder your own fate and opportunity's without knowing it. Sometimes finding out about the past life by astrology or Hypnotic regression can reveal and release the karmic block and leave the road clear for money to come you by whatever means are destined.

If you owed debts to people in former existence, you may have to pay them first in this life, before you can gain wealth. The debts can sometimes be paid back by service work, caring work, contributing something rather than money. If you are person who has given nothing to others in any form in this life, this might be a way of redeeming the karma and paying past debts so money can some to you.

Misuse of money

If your generous because you want to be loved or made popular, it may be in the past life you " bought, bribed or tried to use money to coerce or persuade people into doing what you wanted, or into being what you wanted them to be. Money may have been the only value you knew. In the present life money may be with held until you learn self value, and to value others for who they are, so that people can love you for who you are., not what you have or what you give them. Or so you can stop trying buy and manipulate people with money. Learn to love yourself, without having to have others reinforce your ego. Love yourself with you aesthetes and your shortcomings, the good and bad in you, stop selling yourself and demanding popularity in exchange for money or demanding that others falter or feign love for you with subtle or secret payments to induce them to do so.

Working With Your Chart To Gain Wealth

The First and Fourth House.

Much of the book is about overcoming obstruction to wealth in one's psychology or karma, because in doing so, it is like opening the locked door of a safe, so that money which is already piled up on the other side waiting can fall into your life There is often no need to do anything else, yet these tasks of unlocking that have been present through out the book can be the most difficult. Everyone wants an instant formula for getting rich. A series of numbers to win the lottery. It is difficult to write a book about money that is also spiritual, because people refuse to connect the two and have trouble thinking of them as one and the same. This book can make you rich, perhaps not instantly, but it will do so, and it will, also make you a better person spiritually, which is true wealth.

Negative thoughts reflected in the first or fourth house of you chart, can refer to over identification with ones background. Or with a beginning of hardship. The first house of the chart symbolizes you beginning is life, and the fourth house, your background a roots. Difficult planets in these areas of the chart means a difficult beginning or problems stemming from your background. This can create a mental blocks, when trying to get on, things like thinking of the impossibility of becoming rich, because you had a background of few privileges and early imposed financial limitations, things you had no control over, the circumstances of birth, for example being born into a poorer level of society, an underprivileged class or cast. Let go of your mental blocks, negative thoughts of the impossibility of becoming rich or rising, the self imposed financial limitations of, class consciousness. These include a lack of sophistication or learning, Shyness, self consciousness of working class accents, or clothes, or lack of influence that keeps us on one level in life or other. There are many unconscious limitations in character, that impose on us the fate we expect financially at every turn in life.

Whether we expect a bargain in a shop, or insist to pay the highest price thinking that costly is quality. If we expect to have to work for all we get, or expect something for nothing, they are all potential blockages. Things that hem us into a small limited world, on our own small level, So do things like, feeling undeserving, feeling shabby or poor. A true lack of emotional self worth, and self defeat, under valuing yourself puts you in a down ward spiral materially. One level inter reacts with the other. Mental blocks, and low self worth end up as financial blocks that stop money coming in.

The astrological villains for those kind of thinking are Saturn in the first house. Or afflicting the Sun,. Saturn afflicting the ascendant by aspect. Shyness, inhibiting self conscious of one background can be the Moon in the first house. An afflicted Mars in either first or fourth, Or Mars afflicting the cusp, can make it hard to believe in ambitions, or in the possibility of getting on in life. If neither the first or fourth house receive any good or encouraging aspect or have good planets in them, the background and circumstance of ones birth do not help us rise, or belief that we can, even though circumstance are not nicely bad or lowly. Curiously Venus a good planet in the fourth house, even when well aspected is not conducive to rising in life or gaining wealth either, but for different reasons, the person is usually happy with their birth circumstance and doesn't have enough motivation to get on, even if they would like to have more.

A belief that life is hard, will make it hard. So will under valuing yourself emotionally. We all create our own reality to some extent, All the things that impoverish you emotionally are likely to act in some way to skin you further financially. If a person doesn't feel good enough, for the job he applies for, or thinks it uncomfortably above his social level. He wont be at his best at the interview, and his success is distracted from, again creating the downward spiral of poverty and failure to rise in life in that area. If you hold onto such beliefs and limitation long enough they end up materializing, one by one as poverty, loneliness, misery, miserliness and lack of spiritual well being. You may then feel such beliefs are justified, that they are telling you the truth about life, that you cannot get anywhere, but all you have done is to construct a set of self limitations and self limiting ideas, a personal mythology of poverty and failure.

As you change those ideas you break through the wall, you send out a better kind of message, you move onto a slightly different path of fate You become more open to receive money. Before you can receive it, you have to release what's old and outworn dowdy in your life, especially mental attitudes as these things create the poverty consciousness.

Making Your Chart Work for You

Assess the strengths of the houses. The computer will usualy do this for you, but you can do it yourself. How do we determine if a house is strong? For those not familiar with this form of astrology. A house becomes strengthened when it is linked with other important features of the chart. There are exceptions but in general, the following is true,

Angular houses, especially the first house are generally considered stronger than the other house in a chart. Empty houses with no planets in them are weak and can be discarded. Intercepted houses are weak and can be discarded. A planet in "determinant " is weak. Detriment is when a planet is in the opposite sign to the one it rules. For example Saturn is in detriment in Cancer. Retrogrades are also weakened planets, though they are not called detriment.

An angular house with no planets will be stronger than other houses with no planets.

Look mostly to the occupied houses. A house that stands out because it has a stelium or large number of planet in it, is usually regarded as strong. An angular house with a stelium would be stronger than a different house with the same number of planets in it's stelium. So in this way we begin to weight the strengths of the houses in the chart against one another, to find the strongest.

The house where your Sun is, or your ruling planet is usually regarded as strong. So if your Sun was in the first house, it would have two strengths, one for the Sun, one being angular, if it had another planet there, so long as that planet was not in determinant it would have three strengths, a score of 3, set against all the empty houses, angular or not who would have a score of zero. Naturally not all the other houses are going to be empty, so you need to add them on their own merit. You need to find the house with the highest score in the chart. This is the strongest house. In the chart.

The meaning of strengths

The Eleventh House is strong. In the financial chart it shows that wealth can be achieved through the tenth house. That is recognised achievements. Of the self, the ambitions and Career goals. Not necessarily the Career you find yourself in now, but the Career that has elements or approximates to what you most want. The strong eleventh house gives the power to make money from some work desired, even if it is in a disguised or twisted or different form from what was originally wished for.

The Fourth House suggest that one day you'll will gain wealth though property investments, or gain a valuable property. It describes your roots, your heritage and your private life. Home ownership may be a subconscious priority in your life and may became a reality early on. Your house is your wealth. You would also become richer in your own city, or country, rather than abroad or in a distant one..

First house strong, and you will gain money by self employment, By your own efforts and own talents and by the force of your character and personality.

The difference between success and failures sometimes chance. If your fifth house is strong, chance will determine many things in your life. Great luck and great disaster, depending on the rest of your chart. With Astrology we can help create own luck and chances. Even if an unsuitable fate seem stacked against us, we may not be able to totally overthrow it but we all have the power at least to improve it.

When the Eighth House has strength in your chart. It is the house of ancestry, inheritance, death, legal matters, and metaphysics. With this house strong there are sometimes legacy or money properties and goods handed down, on the deaths of family or friends or benefactors unknown. Though these cannot be counted on for wealth as the number of times one receives a legacy in ones life is rare. With the exception of those who work with the dying or elderly and even them such legacies are usually not very great but are more gifts or appreciation.

Power of prayer

A client was walking in the city of London. She rested her feet on the steps outside St Paul's cathedral. She had no substance in life, not much money in her pocket. She happened to pass the Bank of England, the famous old woman of Threadneedle Street. The "Cathedral of wealth". This thought entered her mind looking at the small historic and yet beautifull stone building. At one end of the bank building; it had tall stone pillars like a Greek temple. Supporting a kind of portico, and on the ground under this, is a kind of paved circle shape. Impulsively she stood in the centre of the circle, and said a prayer. Being the bank she prayed for some money, for finances to be better. Half in jest, half in earnest. Just one of those wild impulsive youthfull things we do sometimes without much thought, it just seems right or instinctive at the time. A few months elapsed, and in the year that followed, she received several sums of money, large enough to make a difference.

I no longer have the woman's chart but It came to me in an illumining moment that there are temples of every kind, hallowed places of every kind. Some places get hallowed over the years simply because of the thoughts and incidental prayers and desperations of people going there, create a kind of vibration that may be a positive energy that rises up to the gods. In the same way that churches become hallowed, over the century's Imagine everyone going to the bank manager in a thousand banks in the country for a loan, they are saying in their heads, " please god let him give me that loan, I need it so badly. " And the bank of England London, maybe the most powerful money temple in the whole of England the cathedral of money in. It could be coincidence, but in astrology we learn that all things are connected.

But many years later my client found herself in London, and again walking in Threadneedle street. The memory returned unbidden, so she traced her footsteps to the Bank of England and said two prayers. One of thanks, and one of asking. And again that year her life changed more subtly, but in a deep way; her direction altered financially. She knew I was writing this book and wanted me to tell her story, but anonymously, it's like a gift, a giving back to the God of Money, for what else did she have to offer, but love and a humble promise to tell as many people as possible.

Some religions tell us not to prey for money, that's is linked with selfishness greed, desperation and evil, that money corrupts. And is at the root badness, like a poisoned vine. I disagree. We prey for the restoration of health to others, ill health corrupts the body's of those who have no defence, death takes the good from our lives, but poverty can also corrupt and corrode people lives and it can do so as much as wealth. We prey for own healing, we prey for those who are sick, or in desperate situations, and peril, we prey for damaged tormented souls and we prey for own enlightenment and for our soul to be saved and be shown the way, so why not prey for money, if money can help make things better for us and others.

Money can save us or enlighten us, if it will pay for our university education, for our house to be warm and have the roof that doesn't leek. It can free us from slavery so we have time to think and live instead of work and struggle. An advanced soul can do immense good, more with money both for itself and others than it can without money. An evil soul will do evil regardless of whether it's rich or poor.

Money, greed, desire and some people who have it, may have created some of what is wrong with the world today, which is maybe what some of the old religions were warning us about. But money has a peculiar alchemy in the experience of life, it. can be both the poison and the antidote.

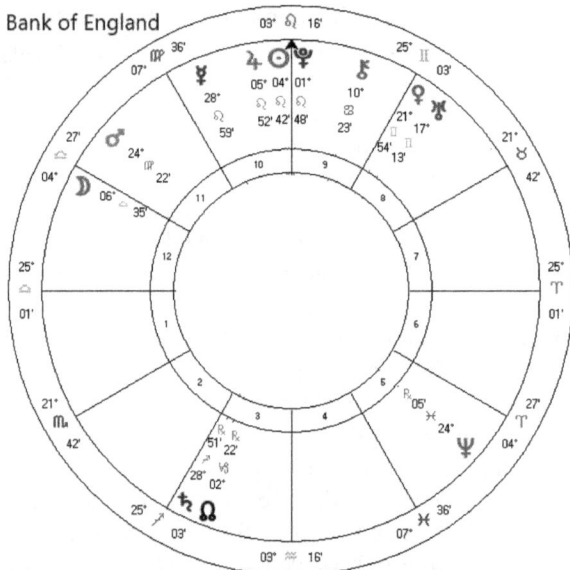

Bank of England

Everything is worth a try, let your intuition guide you to the right place at the right time, and let your soul speak, let your heart and motive be pure and open,, free from greed, corruption or bad desire if you can, let your prayer or wish be instinctive and sincere, a thing of the moment, not forced or contrived.

174

If you are in London, pray in the temple outside the Bank of England, as my client did, and then say another one inside the Bank's Museum on the seat between the second pillar and third pillar, for the pillars are like the houses of the horoscope and the second house is money prey naturally and faithfully open your soul and your intent to fate and destiny and the gods of money and maybe you, find the answer. If you are in any other place in the world, then let your soul guide you to find the money temple there.

Corrective actions

Many times a chart will indicate a future loss of funds, an example is a malefic transit to the second house Whether you consider the future loss to be due to misfortune, a conspiracy of bad circumstance in your life, or whether you consider it to be due to owing a karmic debt that is being extracted by fate. The way to control loss, is to lose on purpose, to give, in this way we help others while repaying our own karmic debt.

The karmic challenge of gain, is to use the wealth one has received well, and correctly is that our wealth damages no one, including yourself. To quote or misquote an old saying. What will you profit if you gain the world but lose yourself in the process. Wealth can give to us and it can take away from us. Let us try and ensure that our future wealth is gain in every sense of the word. Gain in soul gain in money.

Past life debt

The karma of debt can exist, when a member of family, usually a sibling or an adult son or daughter becomes a burden a wastrel who wont contribute to the household, wont work.

This, is sometimes a Childs karma. A soul who in their recent past life was a child or a dependent soul with everything provided for nothing. Everything given. But a child who died before adult hood, or working age, when he would have had to learn to take financial responsibility for himself and to earn everything he got, and also pay back the family who looked after him as a child by looking after them. So a part of the character did not grow up. The person reaches a stage in the present life and regresses or gets stuck in that child phaze.

Alternatively it can indicate earlier older lives spend as a beggar, or vagrant enjoying freedom, but being supported by others. Or life in a communist country, where the state provided everything, and no one had to pay for electricity or rents, A spirit who failed to equate work with payment. (in communism the state provides for you, but you provide for the state by working so I the end you still only get what you earn) In past lives such a soul did not learn to pay his way. Wanted more than he earned. Settled too easily into idleness, chronic unemployment in this life. Fell into a pattern of debts and borrowing or being a burden on the family. In this life he may have to learn hard lessons from bankruptcy, loss of family support, at some point he will be thrust on his on his own feet, starting again, so that he eventual learns to pay his way, and to live on what he earns and behave like an adult in this life. A life that will be very hard and without luxury, until he learns the lessons his soul needs to grow. It is not a punishment, more a fate of evolvement. So his spirit can progress.

Occasionaly a mature hard working adult soul, will also slide into debt, despite his best efforts to avoid it and to pay his way. It will seem that fate conspires against him. Such karmas can be very personal and individual. But usually temporary. They can only be interpreted and corrective advice given from examining the persons own chart.

Past life debts karma, can include either Luna South Node in the second/ eighth house axis. Particularly if they are conjunct Saturn. Neptune or the Moon in the second house, and aspected to the ruler of the eighth house.

If wealth came too easy in a previous incarnation, and was not appreciated, understood or was wasted it may be harder gained in this one, so that it's lessons can be integrated into the soul. (Jupiter aspects, linked with karmic aspects) If you were responsible for plunging others into debt and deep suffering in past lives (Mars, Pluto's). Or miserly, mean selfish and over retentive. refused to help others in dire circumstances (Saturn). These karmas need to walk many steps in the shoes of the struggling and destitute the outcast to understand the same misery in this life. So money luck wont change until we have at least endured a few steps A way of off setting such karma can be to make a career working with or for the poor, or to work free in a charity to alleviate such conditions. In healing our own individual karma we go beyond our self and heal the karma of the world. What the soul needs to learn is kindness, generosity sharing and unity with humanity, instead of separateness. When the soul learns that we can all be poor together we can all get rich together, but we are not separate from each others destiny, or each others suffering, then new wealth will come into your life.

If you owe money, give sincere thanks for each debt and the person owed. Do not resent or hate the people or banks, or authorities, or loan sharks you owe money to, even if they are pressing for it. They have been good enough to loan you money when others did not, or to give the goods that you owe money on, when others would not. Silently ask Fate or the powers of universe, or the Gods that you believe in to make them prosper, and to make you prosper too, so you can begin to pay back what you owe, each payment you make is a foot step towards wealth and a foot step away from the ties of debt that prevent wealth

Traps of religion

The spiritual conception that money is bad or evil, that one must not desire it. Is an incantation of self denial. It is a common teaching in many religions. You must re educate you subconscious, I always say to people, you have two legs, you walk. You. Would not think of hopping everywhere instead. There are two wheels on a bike, both work in tandem. Recognise that the material and financial side of life is equal and as important as the spiritual side. To live for one and not the other is like hopping on one leg instead of walking on two. Or like riding a one wheeled bike. There is spiritual and there is material, don't think of abandoning one for the other, you must use both in balance. Other religious tenets are The " good" don't become wealthy or if they do they give it all always for good works. If a person has a guilt complex or feels something about them is wrong or sinful to begin with, then the mind that believe this and dictates the path of fate will unconsciously choose, a poor and struggling path. There are two psychological reasons here, one is the desire to be accepted and in religion your only accepted if you become good, therefore subconsciously from an early age the mind is made to think that having little wealth or giving it to the needy or greedy helps one become good. The conscious mind may desire wealth, but the unconscious is still looking for acceptance and freedom from guilt so it steers you down a fated path of poverty

In order to make money you have to free yourself from these old myths of childhood to help the deeper subconscious to detach itself from negative threads of the past, for such threads become prison bars things like guilt and paying for ones sins, an hardship being good for the soul, and other notions that perpetuate poverty. Otherwise we become self punishers, directing our own fate to the poor path, when we could just as easily take the wealth path. A richer world is a better world for everyone. A belief that it's human nature to struggle and suffer, whether it comes from religion or your background will also keep you anchored there, it will justify your poverty and suffering instead of freeing you from it and Hinder your ability to change life. If you hold onto such beliefs subconsciously for long enough they will soon end up materializing, as deeper poverty, loneliness and loss, You may then feel such beliefs are telling you the truth about life but all you have done is to put up and perpetuate a set of self limitations and self limiting ideas. You reap what you sow, and as you change those ideas you start sending out a different kind of message or instruction to your subconscious, you move away from that trap onto a slightly different fate path which in time will materialize as greater wealth and happiness. Another antidote to religions subconscious psychological notions is to carve out a good path to wealth, one that does not add to your sins or imagined sins and spiritual debts and is as beneficial to others as it is to you.

Sun in First House

Many people with the Sun in the Radix First House become self employed, or become important and have great personal wealth during their life time, even if they start off poor. With this Sun, you will gain enough money in the course of your life to become independent and become the master of your own destiny. This may take time. But the long term security and finances in your life will come to depend entirely on your own efforts. You will become self sufficient at the very least and immensely rich at best. The next step, and this belongs to more advanced astrology book, is to calculate when this wealth and self sufficiency will happen, which part of your life.

Sun in second house

This is less fortunate, traditionally it means you will waste some of your money. By transit the Sun in the second house highlights financial matters but can also bring loss of money, financial stringency, and advises you to put of financial decisions untill next month, when the Sun will have moved on and away from that house/.

Sun in Third House

Your earnings and income will eventualy come from commercial activity's or exchanges, short journeys, new meetings and perhaps from intelectual or written work. Communication plays a key role in your life. You experience a continual thirst for knowledge and an equal urge to let others know what you have learned. Your siblings may be important to you

Sun in Fourth House

Some of your earnings or aesthetes in life will come from property and real estate, Investment in the purchase of house or a property. There is always the capacity to work from home. Your home and family are paramount. How you fit into the family and your role and position in the family are of major importance to you. You learn most about true yourself in the family environment.

Sun in Fifth House

Your earnings will either be linked with leisure activity's, sports or the arts, or else you are likely to invest and spend money in this area. You express yourself through fun and creativity. You like to play. Your urge to learn about yourself through creative projects is strong. Children may also be important in your life.

Sun in Sixth House

It is exclusively from your work, activity's, tasks and efforts that you will earn money or make a profit. But you should expected amount to be limited. In addition this placement of the Sun, sometimes means money being spent on health matters. Daily routine, health and work are the areas in which you shine. You will learn life's lessons through your ability to serve.

Sun in Seventh House

Agreements and contracts or associations of some kind will probably determine the nature of your income. This placement of the Sun is also fortunate for a wealthy marriage or earnings and gain from spouses. Relationships are the arena for your self knowledge. Your intimate partner will become your mirror providing a reflection for self-knowledge. Business partnerships may also be prominent

Sun in Eighth House

At some stage in your life you will get an un-hoped for windfall. You will also get bonuses, you will gain by legacy's, settlements, marriage, Social Security payments and by hand outs, borrowing and presents. External resources are of importance in your life. With this sign the spouses and partners usualy do not live as long as yourself. It is therefore good to have them insured. It gives a deep interest in metaphysics and spiritual things. It also means that the financial prosperity will increase after marriage. This sign has a special significance for writers and creative people, it sometimes means that fame for literature, philosophy or intelectual projects comes after death. Or that fame gained in this life time, will last long after your death. There will occasionaly be a sudden and definite financial loss and radical change in relation to your income

Sun in Ninth House

It is in you own interest to make sure your earnings, income or profits are legal, the Sun here can means illicit gains, or risk of ending up on the wrong side of the law. Travel, foreign cultures, religion, and academic studies may provide your keys to the gain of money and higher-knowledge. Philosophies will be explored for self learning. I hope you enjoy the philosophy of money expressed in this book.

Sun in the Tenth House

You gain financial independence or a secure excellent income thanks to your own hard work and your competence When the Sun is in the tenth house, money comes so long as you work for it. The career and advancement in position should be your goal. If you seek fame for yourself or your work this position of Sun will help you find it. You can keep nothing hidden, for this reason it pays to be honest, irreproachable and above board. Your work will shine in public. Profession reputation and standing become the way which you will express yourself and gain wealth in the world. You are ambitious, hard working, good at what you do, and always have one eye on the main chance. You can rise steadily in life, once you find your true vocation, and feeling of purpose. When it comes to poverty unemployment and lack of incentive is your worst enemy, more so than for most people. You tend to desire immediate success, which is not always possible. You get yourself noticed. Money comes. The Sun is at it's highest point in the sky when in the tenth house, and symbolically means you also can rise to the highest point of your Ambitions and fate within your own life time. You can see your dreams of wealth and status come true.

Sun in Eleventh House

In the house of hope, means your greatest dreams will include wealth. But your earnings and income may at some stage depend on the achievement of a project, and also on friends and acquaintances and society's that you belong to, they may be instrumental in your climbing the ladder. You will attain sound and balanced financial resources and support. Your self-knowledge and financial know how will be added to by groups, clubs, and friends. You will also have a strong need for a personal goal and vision. You believe actively in charity and may have a vision of how money and power might help improve the world or your community. At some point in your life you could become involved in fund raising. But you may also be tempted to squander your own money on good causes and good people and impoverish yourself in the process. You are neither grasping or selfish or materialistic about wealth. When poverty does hit you, you have the ability to rise up like a ghost from the ashes of life. You will make a lot of money through internet, computer and global networks, through contacts and communication, and mixing with people. If there is a set back in your earnings it will come early in life because your ideas are often too far ahead of their time. Reviving old money making ides you had in the past can make you rich but timing is everything for you. Gold and precious stones appeal to you, especially to female with this Sun. So does investing some of your money in valuable items, like antiques, wines, manuscripts, works of art, things that may accrue wealth. You waste or fritter a lot of money on friends and social life, and entertaining, and you loan money to others.

Sun in Twelfth House

When the Sun resides in the twelfth house at birth. This placement relates to earnings acquired through difficult, discreet, secret or mysterious work and means, it can also point to inadequate resources, seldom having as much as you need or want. Making money successfully behind the scenes is usually possible, for example, a mail order business, working in a backroom, away from the public view. Or working anonymously, secretly or "under cover " under a name or identity that is different from your own. Your personal identity is hidden or lost in the masses with this sign, even if your work stands out, you wont, and this is how money is best earned an obtained for you. In the twelfth house your money or way of obtaining it is invisible to others. You also experience a deeply-felt connection with the masses., with the financial state of the world economy or community you live in. If you live in a poor community, you will feel at one with poverty and struggle, if in a rich one, you will feel the whole world is wealthier. With this astrological placement, you should surround yourself with the wealthiest people, and best places, do things in as much style and richly as you can, this way because of your subconscious connection with the undercurrents of what's around you, you will develop the mind set to become rich. It will speed your path to wealth. Equally avoid the places and trappings of poverty, the slums the deprived area, the destitute and down trodden and shabby, the cheap and the sleazy. Raise your sight and your spirits and you will gradual increase your money without realizing it untill one day you look back and see the world you have left far behind.

Aspects of a Sun

If your Sun was conjunct the part of fortune in your radix chart. This is a wonderfull aspect, it endows you with a certain powerfull personal charisma. So that you exercise an influence over others and over life itself without even trying to do so. It gives a capacity to make your own wishes come true. So that what you want in life can usualy be achieved. It also brings luck Fortune favours you.

13 Rules for Borrowing money.

How to use astrology to get the bank or the boss to say "yes". Borrowing From your Father, Boss, an Authority who and How to ask.

Rule 1

Your are more likely to receive a loan, if your choose a time astrologically when your own ruling planet or the Lord and ruler of your ascendant is in a good aspect to the lord ruler of the tenth or eleventh house by transit. This is because the tenth house rules your father, your boss, or any person superior by opposition age or standing who has power over you and the eleventh house is that persons money or funds, a good transit aspect means he looks favourable on you at that particular time and the fate between you is good then.

Rule 2

If there are no afflictions or bad aspects at all from transits to the tenth and eleventh house and their rulers, then success is even more certain.

It is not always possible to wait untill all aspects are perfect to request a loan, If there are bad aspect to the tenth and eleventh from other transits, or mixed aspects, say bad aspect to the tenth and eleventh, but these are off set by good ones between your ruling planet and the ruler of the tenth or eleventh, there may be disappointment or refusal, or more likely success in obtain the lone or partial success but after difficulties.

Rule 3

If your ruling planet and ascendant ruler are in a bad aspect to the tenth and eleventh, and their rulers, then a disappointment or a refusal of help is likely to be the answer to your request. The same, if you try to borrow money when the ruling planet, lord of your first house, or your zodiac sign ruler is retrograde. Retrogrades advise you that now is not the right time, but the same request if asked later on when the planets are no longer retrograde may be granted.

Rule 4

Equally if the ruling planet turns retrograde or become stationary just after the loan is granted, or seems about to materialize in your life, do not pin all your hope on it, there is a chance it may be withdrawn or recalled, or very much delayed. That the lender may change his mind.

Rule 5

The Moon in a bad aspect to Mercury, at the time of making a request for money often brings partial disappointment or rebuff. Misunderstandings, or wrong meanings are read into the request. The person may suspect your motives are not genuine, or that your request is foolish, depending on the signs involved. Mercury in Scorpio for instance, and Moon in Taurus hidden motives are suspect, while when Mercury is in the opposite sign of Taurus, the person can be stubborn and inflexible in his mode of thinking and this can make him refuse the request and the Scorpio can give him along memory to something in your past that reflects badly on the request. Aries, too hasty a request, Gemini the person suspect double dealing, lies or dishonesty and so on. The same two planets move quickly so bad aspects can be avoided sometimes by waiting a day or so, untill like a stormy sky they have passed over, and the new prospects are brighter.

Rule 6

Even a good transit aspect may not completely nullify a bad radix aspect. The transits only mitigate the natal chart, and show the best time to make a request for money. They improve on what is there sometime wonderfull, but they cannot guarantee it will always work.

Rule 7

The fewer afflictions the greater the chance of success, when requesting a pay rise, loan, or gift. The same astrological guide lines given above apply to asking for any kind of financial help from other sources. The ruling Lord of your ascendant and your ruling planet always represent yourself. But the house and ruler that represents the people or authority's you are pleading for money change. So use the same rules with the following houses.

Rule 8

Asking your Mother, your landlady, your mortgage company for money; The same rules, but using the ruler of the fourth house and the fifth house to represent the money you hope to gain from the mother, the mortgage broker, the landlord. The fourth house also represents the council or state if you live in a state owned house, and are applying for help towards the rent.

Rule 9

For loans from Brothers, sisters, neighbours cousins, Uncles and Aunts; Use the third and fourth house and rulers. If you have Jupiter in your sixth house at birth, Uncles and Aunts may be favourable to you financially, or may leave a legacy to you after their death.

Rule 10

University and educational and school grants. Research grants and funding. Welfare grants for school uniforms. Buss and Travel passes, and claiming travel expenses. The third or ninth house.

Rule 11

Borrowing from a close friend, a club or society which you belong to, The eleventh, and twelfth house rules.

Rule 12

A lover. Mistress, former marriage partner, or business partner. The seventh house and it's ruler

Rule 13

Compensations claims. Accident claims. If the claim is on an insurance policy, or if the person had died in an accident, the eighth house, the house of death and inheritance will be involved. If the person is yourself and the accident is a traffic or motor accident, choose the third house rulers

If a house insurance claim, use the ruler of the fourth house. A claim against the state, for example falling over an uneven pavement the fourth house. Car insurance, the third, travel insurance the ninth.

While medical mistakes made in clinic and hospitals are twelfth house. Shops and supermarkets are the second house, a fall in them, may involve Saturn or Neptune aspects. Saturn being the planet of fall, and Neptune being the planet of things not seen, liquids, slippy surfaces and fruit skins

Compensations claims for damage or deformity due to toxic chemicals or drugs taken by your mother before your birth, the eighth house. If you are claiming for your child, then use the ruling planet of the child's eighth house, because this is the house of inheritance, including genetic and toxic inheritance, the house it is situated in your own chart, so if the child for example has Neptune in Sagittarius in the eighth and was born with a defective limb due to poisons, you look to the house Sagittarius occupies in your chart, and use that house, and it's ruler Jupiter, along with your own ruling or rising house ruler to plot a good time for making the claim, or brining the court case.

Borrow Money from a Relative?

If you wish to know if you will be successful in borrowing money from a particular relation, take the house in your radix chart that represents the relative, and the next house to it, to symbolise his or her money. For example your mother is the fourth house, so the fifth house is her money. Take the ruler of these two houses, and see where they are transiting in your radix chart. If the transiting rulers are in good aspect to your house of money, or it's ruler, or to your eleventh house, or it's ruler, or to your Sun, or your second house or it's ruler, and not afflicted, then there is a good chance you will be successful. If the planet ruling the relative and his money are in good order and not afflicted, weak or retrograde. But if these planets or rulers are in poor aspect with the planet signifying the relative, or the relatives significator is weak or afflicted or retrograde, then wait untill the aspect is better before you ask, because then the circumstance surrounding the relative will be better.

If in addition to the good aspects listed, if the transit Moon is in favourable aspect to the ruler of your second or eighth house, the prospects of success are magnified. But if the ruler of your eighth house is weak or afflicted or retrograde in it's transit, it means the relative may be willing to help but doesn't have the money to lend at this time so again it is best to wait of you can. Of the transit rules of the eighth house is strong but conjunct the transit or radix Sun, or combust a sit is called, the relative may have the money but it is tie dup or so placed that you cannot withdraw it, or not without penalty, even if the relative is willing to loan it.

If the two rules by transit are going into a square or opposition to each other, or to the ruler of the second or eighth house, the attempt to borrow may give offence. Or there will be a quarrel over it, or if in mutual reception the relatives wealth will be feeble, he or she may be willing to lend it, but doesn't have it, or is unable to summon it.

Debts and their resolution

To answer questions about the outcome of a debt. The first house of your chart represents yourself, and the seventh house represent the person or company you owe money to, or borrowed from in the past. If a meeting, court case, or revue of the debts is due, those are the house in your chart that will provide the judgement on the question. If the ruler of these house are making a good aspect to each other by transit, an agreement or outcome will be reached that under the circumstance is favourable. If a benefic planet is transiting through the first house, or aspecting it's ruler, the outcome is favourable to you, or at least not as unfortunate as you fear. If a benefic is transiting through the seventh or favourable aspecting it's ruler, the outcome of agreement is more favourable to the other party, than to you, but is not necessarily bad or dire for you. If Uranus, Neptune, Pluto or Saturn or Mars afflict the ruler of the first house, the people you owe the money to will have the upper hand in the outcome. If these planets are in the seventh house they can force you into ruin or into legal actions or bankruptcy proceedings.

Asking for a pay rise

There is always an auspicious and equally an inauspicious time to do things. Success can sometime be as simple as timing. To obtain an increase in wager, imagine that the ruling planet of your house of money represents yourself. The ruling planet of your tenth house is your boss or your company. The eleventh house is the house of hope and wishes. If the ruler of your second house is in good aspect to the ruler of your tenth or eleventh house by transit. It is a favourable time to obtain a pay rise.

If the ruler of your first house or your second house ruler is transiting your eleventh house and not afflicted, or retrograde in it's transit, and the ruler of the eleventh is in mutual reception, that is in your first or second house and unafflicted, you will obtain your wages increase. But if there is no good aspects o mutual reception between these two rulers you will not get more wages. And if the ruler of the tenth and eleventh afflict the ruler of the first and second, or one or other is afflicted by a malefic, or retrograde, it may be better not to ask, as the wage rise will not be forthcoming and there could in addition be some aftermath or bad consequence for asking. It is better to wait untill the planet are in a more favourable or auspicious aspect before proceeding.

Aspects from Transits

Saturn/Pluto

This transit is about heavily sustained work and effort to achieve an important goal. Scandal in your life, if you do not do what is right. An advise to work for the common good as well as your own, otherwise there will be reverberations. Avoid becoming a work aholic for the sake of money, and avoid fanaticism and obsession. Let go of things in your life which have ended and which belong to the past. Under this transit old financial secrets can be dredged up. A good aspect for treasure hunters but a bad one for people with something to hide.

The conjunct and the opposition, the square and quincunx, have the strongest effect in that order. Though the conjunction is more positive in outcome.

The house in which the planets are give a clue as to the financial area of life involved. If one of the planets is in the tenth, the financial matter is to do with Career, if in the second, money itself, your debts and wages, the eighth influence over you money, such as the affairs of your boss, company. The twelfth house, the state of the country, the fourth the financial matter has to do with home or property, and so on. Usualy the house of the Natal planets house is the key or foundation of the issuer, so for instance if Radix or natal Saturn was in the fourth, the issue would most likely be about property, while the transit planets house is the passing effect, so transit Saturn in the eighth house aspecting Natal Pluto in the fourth for instance, could have the scenario of, death and inheritance, and the gaining or loss of a property through it. When the transit planet is retrograde, the influence reverses, so that retrograde Saturn, transit in the eighth celestial house, aspecting Natal Pluto in the fourth, the influence would then fall more heavily on the eighth house, and the things it represented, instead of property. The death or inheritance. In some instances it can be the same thing almost, but it can also make a subtle difference, or a big difference as to how an aspect is experienced. It is knowing these differences and estimating them correctly that can mean you get hold of the wrong end of the stick, or right end, you can make the prediction accurate and meaningful, or only partly so.

Neptune / Jupiter

The potential for a chance gain in finances, but also when bad aspects are between them, the potential to be deceived or robbed in financial matters

Saturn / Saturn

Changes in the structure of your life. That may lead to financial changes. These will happen as if by fate or circumstance and will seem irresistible.

Saturn / Neptune

An advice to avoid careless expenditure, and frivolous use of money. Things that seem too good or tempting to be true are usualy false under such aspects, so avoid financial entanglement with shady characters and people who make fine or alluring promises to help you obtain money.

Saturn / Uranus

Sudden change, a break through, something that is suddenly completely over and done with and changed. In the eighth house there are often connections with Taxation, tax evasion, or being hammered by the tax man. Welfare benefit fraud and investigation into your financial affairs. This aspect is not good for people working against the state or system.

Saturn / Jupiter

Promise some new success and financial growth, the conjunction brings easier success, the square usually means an obstacle has to be overcome first. In the eighth house bank loaned are sometimes involved in this aspect or legal actions. This aspect in the natal chart can also fore tell a time in the person life when they will visit a place of great poverty or great contrast between rich and poor and be so moved by it all to change their entire philosophy of life or to turn back to a religion or spiritual ideal they held in the past. The act of poverty and wealth totally transforming the person life, while their own financial standing may not necessarily change with it. Even the minor aspects between these two planets often have ellements of being moved by someone's poverty or wealth but with less far reaching effects.

Saturn / Moon

A danger that poverty or money matters will lead to ill health. Emotional limitation imposed by ones background, parents, past. Wasted potential. Shyness that is detrimental to gaining financial success. Take care of your health and your teeth both may become costly. The parents money may also figure in these aspects.

Saturn / Mercury

Arguments about money and contradicting people, will not win you success. You may need to learn some new technical skills to get on in life and improve you financial prospects, when these aspects happen by transit.

Pluto / Mercury.

A new idea and new contacts can be financially beneficial, when these two planets are in aspect

Pluto / Jupiter

an improvement in finance and also in your standard of living

Pluto / Saturn.

slow long term benefits, Bonds, Long term savings schemes and certificates. maturity's of long term investments. You have new skills that can make you more money in future.

Pluto / Uranus.

A desire for short cuts to wealth or success, but chance will play a role as to whether there is success.

Pluto / Neptune

you seek new answers to old problems. You may want something magical or spiritual to happen,. Or intercede on your behalf in financial affairs. Tithes', Prayers.

Pluto / Pluto

You may need to access your own deep inner power so that you can make your financial dreams into reality. Bad aspects can foreshadow a loss of control or power over your own money.

There is always more than one effect of any transit, in this book I am looking only at the monetary effects and even then only a sketch of possibility's amongst those influences, but even so it is a spark of light that will lift the shadows of the unknown and show you a glimpse of the future.

Saturn

Difficult aspects to Saturn in the natal chart may cause you to believe that you must work exceptionally hard in order to have money or raise yourself from poverty. You may end up creating financial wealth, but find that all your days and nights are eaten up by work. There is no time to enjoy your wealth. This can be because Saturn being the planet of duty and seriousness and working until one is to tired not to work. Has subconsciously made you feel you must assume too many responsibility's and burdens, or take on goals that are too heavy and high. Creating true wealth, that is both spiritual and financial wealth, means striking the right balance between work and leisure. Jupiter is Saturn's natural balance. He rules abundance, well being, faith and joy. Jupiter in the chart shows you the area or channel through which you can create wealth, most easily. Therefore if you have difficult Saturn aspects that seem to condemn you to over work. Jupiter's house and sign and aspect may be the key in your chart to finding the easiest way for you personally to make wealth and to balance the difficult Saturn aspects.

The House Next Door

The astrological chart is symbolic of a great wheel. A wheel of fortune that holds secrets. When you turn that wheel it contents fall out. If you have a question concerning money, there are parts of this wheel that hold the answer. The answer is usually found in the aspects and transits in the house next door.

If you have a financial concern about your home, building a new extension, adding an orangey, converting a room to some other use,, the fifth house holds the answer.

Why? Because the fourth house represents all matters to do with your home. The fifth house, is next door to the fourth. Its the fourth house's symbolic "second house", So it represents your homes money! Bad transits or bad radix aspects here tell you that the extension may cost more than it's worth, or plunge you into hard times. Good aspects tell you things will go just fine, it will increase your houses space or value. If good aspects adorn the second house, this new library, orangery or other extension will also make you happy, because the second house, is the fourth houses eleventh house, or what you wish for from your home and it's repairs, it's building work.

If we want to know if it's worth paying for violin lessons, a course in computing, or about a new vehicle we are considering buying. These are third house subjects. So we look next door from the third house, to the fourth house to find the financial clues. In asking about our business, the eleventh house is the business money, and so on,.

Family Money

The Father, the fifth house and it's transits represents his personal effects, his last will and testament. Funeral policy's and life insurances. While the eleventh may show prevailing conditions on his finance when asking him for a loan. The Mother, legacies, last will, effects and goods are the eleventh house and it's transits a the time of demise.

The fourth house, it's aspects and transits traditionally represents the finance of the first sibling. Also the likely consequence of asking this sibling for financial help, or how financial squabbles between the two of you may conclude. Traditionally the eleventh is any inheritances or bequests to you made by this sibling. However my own research shows the third house tends to represent a younger sibling born after you, while the older sibling, born before you, is signified by the eleventh house and his money and financial affairs, the twelfth. The elder siblings death and any legacy's left to you are shown in the sixth.

The sixth house, the money and wills, legacy's of the second sibling. Also money of your own first child, though the twelfth house is the first child's will and life insurance. The sixth house is aunts or uncles, the seventh their money, their receptivity or lack of it when it comes to helping you out, and first house their wills.

The seventh house, is traditionally the third sibling, also traditionally the grandfather. Though I find from my own experience and research the twelfth house more is accurate to signify the grandparents. The second child's financial affairs is also traditionally shown by this house. Business partners have their financial affairs in the ninth, and their deaths in the second. Benefactors, the fifth, anonymous benefactor, the fifth and the twelfth house. This house system is of greater interest to students of astrology who are using this book for study than to those who are simply trying to us this book to improve their wealth quickly, so let's return to the sudden acquirement of money. The big question you are waiting to ask comes next!

Just tell me the winning numbers

You're an astrologer, so why not just predict the winning numbers of the National Lottery for me this week?

This question is often asked in jest by some people, and in earnest by others. It is also used sarcastically by some who anticipate a negative answer and want to use the question to depreciate the value of astrology, or to mock, and unwontedly jibe in at the astrologer. So let's tackle those people first. Let's paraphrase this, would you ask a school teacher if they can make you clever? No? Then why ask an astrologer to make you rich? Think on that. The moment we deride a thing we put a barrier in our mind that limits our understanding and impoverishes our experience of life. So let me now answer this question seriously.

In theory if we can predict other things, then we should be able to predict winning numbers, winning horses, winning anything. I believe we can. Most psychics, astrologers, and occultists get asked this question periodically, in various forms. "If you can predict the future, what about the Lotto, can you tell me the winning numbers this week ? "The first time a new client asked me this it was written like a codicil at the end of her letter, a little quip of an "after thought". I smiled, thinking she was jesting. I made the major mistake of assuming that what is obvious to me is also known by others. People have misconceptions about astrology. I answered her post script in a equally light hearted way. When I get all the lotto numbers right I'll be doing your readings for free!

Much to my surprise she took me very seriously and said that would be Ok! I should have answered her foot-note enquiry as methodically as I answered her other requests. As I came to know Alma I discovered she was the kind of person who was humorless yet naïve and sincere, inquisitive, level headed, with a healthy skepticism and a practical turn of mind that had tight boundary's. She had an interest in Gambling, a good head for numbers and figures and a character and the making of an intelligence that would very likely succeed in devising her own winning systems. This was why she'd asked the question, she did not expect the actual winning numbers to win a fortune, but more a system, a way of calculating. She wanted to know if I knew anything of use that she didn't know and that would help her.

Some people use the same sort of question as a derision to astrologers everywhere. Some ask as a joke, or to offset their own belief in astrology incase you're a confidence trickster, or incase astrology is a load of rubbish, so they can pretend they were not taken in by it, they never took you seriously in the first place. Some ask simply to introduce and ellement of teasing, fun and friendliness into the communication. Yet others real gamblers who believe if there is any chance at all, even a cats chance in hell, they will see if astrology can give them an edge. They don't always believe in astrology or psychics, but they ask on the off chance, that million to one chance that you do actually know, or can use your psychic powers in their favour, and they share their winnings with you if you get it right. For it is true to say that in certain charts one can see things., that are not strictly astrological but come from some inner psychic perception of what's there.

There is a problem in trying with pure astrology to predict the winning series of numbers, for lotterys, raffles, or horse races, or Football matches, or for anything else, The problem is that the fate of masses and millions of people are involved. It is comparatively easy to predict the fate of one person, or one horse. It is also easy enough to look at the charts of say four politicians standing for election and know which one will win, Or to look at the chart of an individual horse and know it's racing future, if it will be a champion, if it will break it's leg, or stumble or if will it throw it's jockey. It is also possible to look at the transit aspect at the time of a particular race, the race and see what that destiny of the horse will have that day. We can say confidently this person or horse will run well, because it shows in the chart, we may also be able see it winning. But If we wanted to be sure it would win, we would have to compare his chart with every horse in the race.

To take the chart of the national lottery and predict a winning series of numbers, would not be practical or possible. In the national lottery, because there are too many factors to confuse and skew the results. The destiny of millions of people. The random and chance factors. Yet maybe it doesn't have to be that complex. Astrology can predict some outcomes, The fact that I have not predicted it, doesn't mean it cannot be done. If we have enough time, and enough information, we do can do much to predict winning sequences.

Early in my career, when I had more time to correspond with my clients, a client who knew something of astrology himself, but only a few scraps, asked me if we could work out a way of predicting how his favourite football team would do in the cup. It was an interesting challenge for me. I suggested that, rather than working with dozens of footballers charts we must devise a method of calling the team one entity, or person, so it had only had one chart to work with. And the same with the opposing teams. In short we had to decide on a "birthday" for the teams. Then his favourite teams success and future could be predicted, much as a persons, or a countries fate, When there was to be a match we treated the two charts like a kind of predictive synastry to decide who would win and what would happen. This worked very accurately, his knowledge of football and mine of astrology combined themselves nicely though the client did most of the work as it was his interest and system, not mine. The significant ellement for me rested on how to decide the teams modern day birthday. Often in this kind of astrology, whether for spots, countries, towns, politics. buildings or other important things, the dates that are historically significant, like when the team began, or when the house was built, or city was founded do not work very well, for astrologically it is like trying to predicting your own future from an ancestors chart.

The method of deciding the teams or games modern day birth date, can be a long process of individual trial and error. To do this you really need to be devoted to the subject, as my client was, and knowledgeable about it. At least with football or baseball teams we always have a birth place that is accurate, that's a start !. Another client was a chess fanatic., wanting to know he results of big games, but unable to find out the opponents birth data. But take heart dear student, when you manage to devise a method that works once as a useable " birth date" for something that was never born, all the labour and deduction and hard work is over, and it will work again., I would encourage you all if you have a great interest in some sport or game (unfortunately I don't, neither do I have an interest in gambling) to experiment with such things, using both your knowledge of the game and your knowledge of astrology. Whatever method you use, astrology, numerology, or some system of your own, Keep trying, Nothing is ever won by giving up.

The astrology of chance is one of the most fascinating and frustrating. Often one can devise systems that bring small wins, but not the one big life time win. Its encouraging, maddening, motivating, baffling or beguiling, because systems come so close, or work once but then cannot be repeated. A system that cannot quite be perfected, teases with it's dance., one keeps returning to it in idle moments in the hope it can be improved. That certainty can made out of chance. Through my own attempts I have gained a different kind of riches, a wealth about astrology and chance, I have gained insights about the holistic quality of attracting wealth that is far more valuable to any astrologer than money, the search for truth is never a wasted journey.

Astrology can tell you when the good aspects bring the most fortunate periods for gambling, for work, for new ventures. It can point you on your own individual path to money, and tell you which numbers, colours, direction and so on are beneficial for you personally and if you follow the advice faithfully you will become wealthier. Any good astrologer will work with your chart and help you maximize the potential for wealth

Take advantage of the lucky transits. The Moon in aspect to Jupiter is lucky for most people. Note any aspects to the ruler of your eighth house, as it's the house of other peoples money, or happy aspects to the fifth house which is the, house of fun and gambling, or the eleventh house, ruling wishes windfalls and gifts, you are Moe likely to have good fortune in gambling at that time.

A fair contest between two or three opponents, for example political candidates at an election, can be judged more easily, than a contest between two teams, or a horse race where there are many runners. If you know the birth date of the two or more political candidates, examine the transits to their charts, and compare both charts Compare that to the national chart if you have one, one contender will clearly emerge the victor. The outcome of a boxing match can sometimes be determined in the same way by chart comparison and the transits at the time of the match. Such a process takes a lot of time and effort, just trying to obtain the birth data, can take time. So can the judgment of the transits and charts, that can take hours, so it is only worth doing if the result is important to you, if it will change your life or your luck to know.

This is true of all astrological gambling systems, they take time and effort. Part of becoming rich is not to waste time on trivial things. If it makes a difference who will be voted the next Prime minister, or which boxer will win the Big fight, then put the effort in, but if you are only going to win a pizza and a drink from your mates, or a small denomination bank notes, and gambling isn't really your hobby, then to work continuously at such systems can be more struggle and effort than the pickings are worth. Time is the most valuable item we have.

Races, Lotteries, Contests

An astrologer friend told me a picture of the winner was always somewhere in the chart. This friend is not wealthy but has moderate success in gambling as a hobby. If you draw the astrological chart for the day and time of the race, then regard the planets as stationary, and in your mind, move the fifth house cusp in a clockwise direction, the same way as stars would move up over the horizon in the sky. The first planet star, asteroid, fixed star or point to which the fifth house cusp makes an aspect holds the secret image of the winner. For example if the first aspect the fifth cusp makes is say a square to Pluto, the name will have a plutonian connotation, if we look to our list of runners names, there may be a "Dark lady" an "Undercover" or a "secret agent" running. All Pluto type names and symbols, The name may often be less obvious then these, and the more knowledge of astrology you have in untangling it the better. If no name seems to fit. Try the fifth cusp next aspect. Make a note of the winners name when the race is over, and re examine the chart to see if you can find a connection. This way you learn to refine your system. The connection of horses to planets and asteroids may seem random, but it is fully in accordance with the traditional rules of astrology.

To choose winning numbers for a lottery by the same system is much more difficult. We can draw up a chart for the time and place the lottery will be drawn, but we cannot always find the way to translate it into numbers. My friend who like me believes in pictures might say if you compare the lottery chart with your own if the transit fifth house, aspects one of your planets, or your fifth house aspects the lotto chart, such a planet or house may give a picture clue to the number. What it really does when it works, is draw out your own intuition by symbolic association.

Keep a record of your efforts at this and all such systems. Your success and failure. After a while you will notice a pattern that will help your system become more accurate. There may be discrepancies, Neptune, Mercury aspects for example when a horse whose name fitted perfectly should have won, but did not. Neptune and Mercury are deceptions. Remember some races are rigged, sabotaged, which means they are no longer games of chance, no longer under the rule of fifth house. Some are just unpredictable. This also should be easy to determine with practice. To become rich it is as important to be able to predict when you wont win money, as when you will. This way you learn what and when to gamble, and when to keep your money for next time.

In any kind of gambling II would always advise an exact orb be used where possible, an orb of more than three degrees can be less reliable in gambling. (For those not familiar with the term orb, an exact orb, for instance if an aspect is in square it's a 90 degree aspect, but in astrology a planet is usually counted as square, even if it is say 93 degrees, or 87 degrees. Some astrologers can work with an orb as far away as nine degrees, bur most allow an orb of only three to seven degrees from the exact true aspect. The number of degree errant of the true, is called the orb)The same method can be distilled for use on other sports and contests and games where there are several contenders and Names are relevant.

When gambling won't bring success

Always take your natal chart into account when using systems of astrological gambling. If you have a bad transit to your house of money or it's ruler, it is unlikely even the best system will work well for you at that time.

If transit Neptune or the South Node are in conjuncting to your eleventh of fifth house. The house of gifts and houses of gambling, then if winning the lottery is your dearest desperate wish, winning it will only prove to be an illusion. You cannot change an aspect, but you can change you wish, so you if this is a radix aspect, your generally not lucky, but more likely to be a winner, when you have some totally different desire in your heart, and less likely when the wish to win dominates your thoughts.

If the ruler of your house of money is opposed by any malefic transiting planet it is certainly not good day for betting, playing for money, or trying to advance your wealth in any easy way.

Beware of people who claim to be miraculous and tell you the winning numbers, or make magic for you for a vastly high cost so you can win that life changing amount. I recall a client who having paid out a substantial sum for someone to do her a ritual, that did not work, said of the Magician " His house didn't look up to much, for a man who charges that amount. It was in poor repair and in a place you wouldn't want to walk through after dark, " This simple human observation says a lot. Be very wary of people who claim to want to make you wealthy, while totally eschewing wealth themselves.

There is no one so holy that they are above money. Holy people, magical people want the world to be a better place, and they know that the right use of money can help make it better. Wealth can buy you freedom from want, it can buy you the time to do what you want, to live in a place where your life isn't made hell, to help who you want, to think and study, or to work without charging for your art or services if that's what you want,, or give to others, if that's what you want. A wise person doesn't live in self imposed poverty or danger. He' is no different from you or me, if he knew the number he'd predict them for himself, have a nice life, and use his new wealth to do his good works. I do not want to include too much of myself in the book, there is already far too much, but one of the questions you will surely ask is,. " Has this system or way of financial astrology worked for me?.

Yes it has, this is why I am passing it on to you. I was born into disadvantage. I would say that happiness was rationed in my life. My beginnings were Stony ground in every way. I lacked education, security, friendship, I lacked a faith to believe in and behind everything else I lacked money. Poverty was the sometimes colourfull, but often drab cloth of my early life. My first interest in astrology was in prediction. Astrology was like a neglected old building and I wanted to restore. Applying astrological rules to gaining wealth came natural, though it was not as interesting to me personally as prediction or medical astrology, it was curiosity about astrology that more motivated me. I did not expect to gain money, when it worked my life gradually changed I had more money than I needed. This was not " wealth" not by your standards anyway, nor by mine now, but at the time it made a difference, because prior to this I had much less than my needs and nothing for my fancy's or my greed's. I continued to research and experiment, I make notes on all things I research, and gathered the knowledge of astrology and wealth and in the process. I continued to prosper. And still do. I gained enough money. Or as much as I needed and wanted to have. None of this was instant, it was a journey Not a "quick fix". It worked for me, and it will work even better for you, for you have a greater hunger in your soul for wealth.

The odd thing I found at was the end of this astrological journey, the more money I had the less it meant to me. You read of people who are so rich as to make billions through business every single minute of their day. You think for a time, How I wish that was me, every dream I have ever had could come true. With astrology all things are possible. But think when you have more money than you could ever possibly extravagantly use up in a life time, than even your descendants couldn't use up. the unusable part of that money, the vast countless wasted part becomes utterly pointless, it may as well not exist. Because it has no tangible meaning. What is the point of making a million a minute? You cannot use a million a minute, not in your lifetime. You cannot experience it in any realistic way, it has less substance less worth than a thought..

Money is exceedingly important, and it is an imperative survival struggle when you don't have enough. The emptier your pockets the greater the value money has. Because money is survival. And anyone who tells you poverty is good for the soul hasn't been below the survival line for long enough!. There is nothing good about poverty Once you have what you need to live on, and even more, money becomes a thing for luxury's. A warm coat has a tangible palpable value, and this is a greedy phaze of gaining, you want this, you want that. you pay more than a thing is worth, you move up, you dress up, you have the best, you have the latest. All the status symbols and the long craved items of desire. The holidays and the luxury life styles, the dream home, whatever you desire. It can seem your thirst for gain is never quenched. Money begins to transform your material life. This is a joyous time, a carefree time, a most wonderful dazzling time. The first phaze is often a Saturn transit, where gain is hard but regular, the second a Jupiter transit

Then when you pass this phaze of luxury and joy and extravagance, and generosity and waste. When you have greater wealth still, you reach a new plateau, money doesn't mean so much, it is still loved and appreciated. Your greed has been satiated, you take it for granted, you will always have it. Your no long interested in status symbols, or showing off to friends, or being generous to friends, the free loaders have gone. The vultures that remain are well fed. Success the best revenge is still nice, but not strived at. It no longer matters much. The lavish life remains sometimes, but the house or car, the brand names, the exotic locations, the things that once seduced and dazzle you, like a mirage in the desert, fade and are replaced with more truly valued material things, the memory is retained because it is a good memory. But the new things work best, the new thing you build into your life are from the core you. This is when Saturn and Jupiter make a favourable aspect to each other. A leveling out.

Somewhere on the journey through the baptisms of wealth and greed and loss and gain, you come into touch with your true self, your inner core, the Sun, or your ruling planet, and you only retain what's really good and practical and, what you want and love in your heart. Money gives you this, the ability to be what's in your heart to be, and do what's in your heart to do and to own what you really want to possess. To go where you really want to be,. To help others, or not to help them. To good in the world, or simply to live your life. Beyond that, hardship is vanquished forever, the wolf is gone, security settles into your spirit, money ceases to matter. Money is a circular journey, the wheel of fortune. It's a spiritual journey, a sacred journey and a fun journey. All journeys have to do with transits in the chart.

Illusions

Why do you want money? More money will improve your life, at least temporarily but it will not solve all problems. If you do not look through the illusion of wealth, you will never really have it. It will all be an illusion, because no matter how much you get it will never be enough.

Avoid living other peoples dreams.

Remember all the lies people told you about yourself. The school teacher, who said you'd never amount to anything. The brother who makes jokes about your lack of money, who's sarcasm cuts like a blade, but is so carefully said so you have no defense. The friend who. Always smirked at his money and your lack of it, and made you feel small. The person who refused you a loan, who said you wouldn't pay it back, when you knew you would and could. The parent who said you were incapable with money, a waster and always would be. The person who made you feel worth nothing, if you had nothing., The many people who proved true the saying, if your pocket are empty you have no friends. The ones who took away your pride, when you had to plead. Wealth can be like a salve to a wound, butt this is all illusion, if you want wealth to show the world that they are wrong, then there will never be enough salve in the universe to anoint that wound, because it's sunk so far into you for so long that it is permanent. All that wealth would be buying you would be acceptance form people you shouldn't care about, because they didn't care enough for you. These same people may even be long gone from your life or dead, but your mind is a haunted house, that cannot leave them behind. Or sees reflections of their nastiness in other newer people. See through the illusion.

See through the illusion of envy and jelousy too. If your vision of wealth is being the glamourous one with the film star looks, who drives the most prestigious car, who has new pent house, every one envy's, and heads turn when you walk across the room. And people half your age with model boy / girl looks fall over each other in hope to spend a night with you, and everyone listens when you talk. If that's you vision of wealth, then your living someone else's dream. You have bought into the stereotype of wealth, or been brainwashed into thinking this is what money is all about. In the past you were envious of someone showy who had the popularity you craved. You still envy it, you want more than that person had, or a bigger version of it. You want to be somebody else. See through the illusion. Until you do you are living not for yourself but for other people.

Some of us only think we want wealth, there may be a fossilized child within us, who wants to other people proud. Or wants not to feel lowly. Maybe he wanted to be the one in the family to do best. Or was jelous of the most popular boy in school the one who seemed, personable, well dressed, all money and streets ahead or above others. Glimpses and envy of a role model, of what you wanted to be. Or maybe you were the child who was always belittled, humiliated, determined to make it big to be better than others. The amount of wealth desired is often in inverse proportions to the amount of worthlessness felt. The roots are long and gather thickness through the years as subsequent events add their portion. Childhood can be long past, but it's spurs can still goad us, digging holes in the future it's incentives still lead us, sometimes painfully in ways we cannot see.

Don't live other peoples dreams, for such is a wasted life.

Want wealth for your own sake, not as compensation for what others or the world has done to you.

Financial advisors

There are certain simple Synastry associations that can help us determine whose advice to take.

If your financial advisors chart, Venus or Jupiter falls in your eighth or second house. He or she will give you profitable financial advice, that will work for you or be helpful for you.

Someone whose Saturn falls in these houses is not good to have as your financial advisor, and someone whose Neptune falls here, may defraud you, or cause you to make costly mistakes.

If the ruler of your twelfth house, is in any way connected to your own financial houses, it spells troubles for you at some stage in the financial association between you. But in synastry if it's also in good aspect to the advisors planets, the person can lead you out of those difficulty's that you sought advice about and away from financial darkness.

Depending in it's aspects to your planets, someone's whose Pluto falls in your financial, houses could help you to find a wealth of financial recourses, or could end up bankrupting you. Pluto is a planet of extremes and can be extremely good or bad.

If the ruler of your house of money is opposed by a malefic transiting planet it is not good day for betting, or for choosing a financial advisor, or trying to advance your wealth in any way.

Balancing the bank

I believe that for everything special, that we are given we should give something back, to maintain the balance of equality and cancel old debts. Don't owe or be in the debt of anyone or anything, if you can help it. If you are in their debt your in their power. Always recall debts owed to yourself by others, if you don't you loss spiritual strength by it so do they. A few years ago, I came down with a kind of flue or chill, that stole my wellbeing and ate at my bones for three days, and. Then I made a remedy from the bark from my tree, and it cured me almost within hours and filled my spirit with wonder and gratitude. Some time past I had read a book that said certain plants dislike certain other plants and wont grow or thrive together. While, other planets are like friends to each other. My lovely tree had nothing growing below it, but this species apparently liked heathers, so I bought the finest most beautiful Scottish white heather plant that I could find, and planted it under the tree to help pay it back for curing me. Both planets thrived.

There is a spiritual currency to such things, that is the same in essence as financial currency's. Life has many strata's like the veins running through rock. To work with wealth spiritually we must also work with the flow and currency of things generally. For wealth is only another balancing of fate.

Whatever our beginnings and roots and whatever our hindrances. we all have a potential for greater wealth that we possess and we all have a chance however remote of being stunningly rich. Wealth is a locked door that can be opened, we just need to find our own personal key, be it though the resolution of karma, Spiritual work, through career, chance, good fortune, talent, or skill; I hope this book has helped you find your gateway to a life enriched and made happy and that, money, freedom from want, and peace and success will reside like a gift in your heart. Thank you for buying my book. May your thoughts on money always be uplifting, and free from deception, greed or falsehood, and may you prosper always

    Ivarna

Rules of Analysis

This may help the reader of the book to use it's knowledge better in assessing the strengths and weakness of the horoscope.

Strong v Weak

If a planet, house, or sign in the horoscope is negative, weak, bad in influence it will act detrimentally or feebly. If positive and strong and good it will influence things favorably or have a prominent effect on life. The following rules will help you decide if a planet, house or sign is weak or strong in your chart. Sometimes weakness and strength can be seen at a glance, at other times the rules will contradict for such is the complexity of astrology, It can be like weighing apples on a scale against a brass weight., it is sometimes hard to tell which is heavier. When that happens you will need to weigh the chart up in greater detail, using in addition the minor rules, or small weights in the scale of rules.

Rule one;

When the ruling planet or "Lord" of a sign, is in his own house or sign it is considered Strong and positive in influence; unless it is retrograde, combust or afflicted by any malevolent planet, which weakness it's strength.

Sun; rules Leo and the fifth house.

Moon; rules cancer and the fourth house.

Mercury; rules Gemini, Virgo and the third and sixth house.

Venus; rules Libra, and co rules Taurus, the second and seventh house.

Mars, rules Aries and the first house. He co – rules Scorpio and the eighth house.

Jupiter, rules Sagittarius, co rules Pisces and the ninth and twelfth house.

Chiron, I have it as ruler of Taurus and the second house. (Other astrologers have their own ideas as to who Chiron rules)

Uranus, rules Aquarius and the eleventh house

Saturn; rules Capricorn, co rules Aquarius, and the tenth house.

Neptune, rules Pisces and the twelfth house

Pluto rules Scorpio and the eighth house.

Rule two

A planet in the opposite sign and house to which it rules is said to be weak, negative in influence or detrimental. For example, Venus is in detriment in Aries and the first house. Because she rules Libra and the seventh house.

Rule three

Exaltation; If a planet is in the sign where it is exhaled it is considered strong.

The Sun is exhalted in Aries; Moon is exhaled in Taurus. North node exalted in Gemini, Jupiter exalted in Cancer, Neptune in Leo, Mercury in Virgo, though some say Aquarius; Saturn in Libra Uranus is Scorpio, South Node in Sagittarius, Mars in Capricorn, Pluto in Aquarius, Venus in Pisces. Chiron in Gemini.

Fall, a planet in it's fall is considered weaker or more negative A fall is opposite to an exaltation. ;

Saturn falls in Aries; Uranus in Taurus; South Node in Gemini. Mars in cancer,. Chiron in

Sagittarius. Venus in Virgo Sun in Libra. Moon in Scorpio North node in Sagittarius. Jupiter in Capricorn Neptune in Aquarius Mercury in Pisces. Neptune in Aquarius.

Rule four

Houses; A house can be considered strong if both it's ruler, and the ruling planet of the house where this ruler is placed are strong. (see above). A house can be considered strong if it's ruler occupies it. Or if it's cusp is aspected by it's ruler or favourable planets. The closer and better the aspect the stronger the house. It is often advisable to disregard minor aspects only use them if for example there is a dispute in your mind over which is the strongest house and need exactness. An experienced astrologer will assess a chart at a glance, without measuring this and that. Don't forget you may not need to know which is the strongest house or sign in the whole chart, you may only need to know if a certain house or sign is strong. You can save yourself much unnecessary work this way. In a money chart you may only need to know if the second house is strong or enfeebled. Or if a transiting planet is strong enough to help your finances.

A house is weak feeble or negative if it is occupied by malefic planets, or aspected by them. If it's ruler is in the house of the rulers fall, or mal aspected.

Too many planets situated in a house are said to weaken it as there are too many energy's pulling in different directions. Though a house with many planet is usually a focus of the person life, bringing the greatest joys or sorrows. So it is difficulty to be sure if this old rule is always correct. It is weakened if it has no planets at all in it.

A house is slightly strengthened if it has it's natural sign on it. For example, Aries is stronger in the first house. Taurus in the second and so on.

Left-overs

These are just a few left overs, crumbs and crusts that don't belong anywhere else, one of the nice things about writing a book that is not commissioned to order by a publisher, is that I can include scraps and scraggs of haphazard information that are of interest to the writer and may be to the reader, but which do not fit neatly into the cupboard or section. Through out the writing of the book, I have jotted such off-cuts into this section.

If the ruler of the first and second house of the chart are in "mutual reception", or in good aspect, the owner of the chart will gain wealth;

Ruler of first house, in second and conjoined with Jupiter, a gain in wealth.

Part of Fortune in the first house, gain by ones own efforts.

Luna node in second, Gain by the occult, by unorthodox beliefs and by money magic is possible.

Jupiter in the second, and free of afflictions and bad aspects, brings Wealth. Jupiter in Capricorn, symbolizes a dislike of waste and tendency to become miserly. Jupiter in Capricorn in the second house then is someone who gains wealth but is ungenerous and frugal with it. While in Virgo they may donate large sums of the gained wealth to charity's.

When the Moon is in the sixth, eighth, or twelfth house from Jupiter, it makes for vast changes in fortune in life. At some point the person may be filthy rich or even famous, at another poor and obscure like a beggar within the same life time.

Pisces is linked with financial dependence. Venus or Saturn Pisces often live lives on hand outs, can be shiftless and dependent heavily on others, and on charity's.

———

Summary

We have looked the positive and the negative in your chart, how you can use your chart to work for you, to attract wealth rather than reject it. How the signs and planets can interact and direct you to making a profit and how to spot the warnings to avoid loss. How the family can manipulate you into following their wishes with promises and bribes. Why poverty breeds poverty, and how to find a way out.

How a small loss can weigh heavily over a lifetime if it is left to fester. Stocks and shares came under scrutiny in where to find indicators of good time to buy and sell. Starting out in business can also be found in your chart, whether self employed or as a company, choosing the right time to start can have a bearing on the success of the venture.

Checking your chart for transits of the Sun, Moon and Jupiter can help you to make the right decisions regarding your finances. We discovered what to look for in the chart before any major decision to avoid mistakes that can cost dearly. Maintaining good Karma was shown to be a valuable asset to a successful life.

Find the Money Box and open up to your wealth, and avoid releasing the poverty parasite. Investigate the House of Inheritance to make financial gains without disturbing the undertaker. Remember success is the best revenge, but be clear about who is to blame, it might be you, use your chart to understand who you really are, and build on your positives. And don't forget the power of prayer, believe it, it works.

Appendix

Here are the basics, find more astrology basics at ivarna.com/faq.

Rulers are planets that have a strong link with particular signs. The rulerships of each house and sign are;

House	Sign	Ruling Planet	Sub Ruler
1	ARIES	MARS	PLUTO
2	TAURUS	VENUS	CHIRON
3	GEMINI	MERCURY	
4	CANCER	MOON	
5	LEO	SUN	
6	VIRGO	MERCURY	
7	LIBRA	VENUS	
8	SCORPIO	PLUTO	MARS
9	SAGITTARIUS	JUPITER	NEPTUNE
10	CAPRICORN	SATURN	URANUS
11	AQUARIUS	URANUS	SATURN
12	PISCES	NEPTUNE	JUPITER

If there twelve planets, each could rule a single sign. But as things stand some rule two signs, some are sub rulers, and the Sun and Moon are lucky enough to occupy a single sign all to themselves.

The quite recent planet, Chiron, I believe rules Taurus, contrary to popular belief, following analysis of my own clients.

www.ingramcontent.com/pod-product-compliance
Lightning Source LLC
LaVergne TN
LVHW091214080426
835509LV00009B/998